All That You Become

THOMAS ROBERTSON

ABOUT THE AUTHOR

Thomas Robertson is a primary school teacher based in Perth, Western Australia. He graduated from Trinity College in 2020, before completing a Bachelor of Education at Edith Cowan University.

At 23, he is still finding himself – learning through uncertainty, discovery and the pursuit of confidence.

His work is grounded in honesty, shaped by his experiences in the classroom and interest in mental health and personal growth.

Outside of teaching and writing, he spends his time immersed in music, with the people closest to him, or simply enjoying the soft moments in between.

CONTENTS

INTRODUCTION

I used to think writing a book was something reserved for those who had everything figured out. I certainly don't.

Growing up, I dealt with comparison, self-doubt and the feeling of not quite fitting in. At times, I felt behind. At times, I felt lost. Most times, I was figuring things out as I went.

Feeling comfortable in your own skin is not instant. It is a journey of ups and downs, of realisations and regrets. This isn't a finished story, but a work in progress.

These pages are moments that shaped how I see the world at 23, along with thoughts I wrote to myself while trying to make sense of it all.

I am not a motivational speaker, nor am I someone who has all the answers.

But maybe you don't need them either.

All That You Become isn't a guide. It's a conversation.

Thank you for taking the time to read this book. I hope it brings you happiness.

With thanks,

Thomas Robertson

CHAPTER ONE
OVERTURE

In 2003, my story began.

A story unfinished - one I hold great pride in.

The reality is, I wasn't supposed to be here.

I was born on the 30th of May in a Patient Transfer Ambulance in Subiaco. My birth came four months before I was supposed to be born, with my due date being in September.

The moment I was born came as a great shock not just for the reason of being premature, but due to my health. I was born weighing just over one kilogram and in poor condition. Six weeks after I was born, my life changed. Due to the complications surrounding my birth, I needed emergency surgery.

Doctors informed my parents of the extreme necessity this surgery held. In what would have been one of the most difficult experiences for my parents, they had to watch their little baby boy go under the knife to save his life. As part of this surgery, I was required to have thirty centimetres of my bowel and small intestine removed. Mum and Dad needed to visit a third hospital for this procedure to take place.

I was given very slim odds to survive this operation.

How slim?

Less than five percent.

It was truly a matter of life and death.

Due to the incredible work and support of the medical staff at Princess Margaret Hospital, I lived to fight another day. My parents had a safe and alive baby boy, the best possible outcome from this uncertain and unreal experience. As a result of this life-saving surgery, I carry a scar on my stomach as well as a small ridge in my nose from an oxygen tube. These are not blemishes or weaknesses, but battle marks reminding me of the greatest fight of my life.

Although I had survived my first major hurdle, the tests weren't over yet. With my four-month stay in hospital came lung troubles, an ileostomy, and regularly changing my stoma bag to ensure proper gut health. As part of my introduction to the world, I also underwent several blood transfusions, x-rays and ultrasounds, at times succumbing to infections and finding feeding particularly difficult.

But all these things were overcome through sheer perseverance and taking each little baby step as it came.

On the 11th of September 2003, I was fortunate enough to be discharged from hospital, having overcome a whirlwind of challenges unlike any I would come to face in later years. My parents were overjoyed at finally being able to relish their own little family.

Not long after being discharged however, I soon came down with a minor form of bronchiolitis and suffered from a hernia, later being admitted to the hospital for more surgery.

However, soon the storm subsided, and I was finally able to be at home, ready to formally take my steps into the world.

In retelling my origin story, I went back and had a look at an old photo album collecting dust on our living room shelf. On the very first page is a letter written by Mum and Dad to the medical staff who helped me survive my initial battles in this world. The letter recounts my journey from birth to arriving home. I took the time to read this letter and doing so was quite the emotional rollercoaster.

Despite not fully remembering these experiences due to how newly formed I was, it still is inconceivable to think I overcame such unexpected and continuous hardship for the initial four months of my life.

Wiping away tears in my eyes, I continued to sift through the photo album. On the initial pages were photos of me in hospital, lying on my bed, bound by medical equipment. On later pages came photos of me at home, enjoying my new-found lucky break. There were also photos of me at my first birthday party which was held at my Nonna's house.

This experience was humbling and moving. The more I turned the pages, the more I realised something vital. In nearly every photo was a family member proudly showing me off to the camera.

Seeing my parents, grandparents, extended relatives and even friends of our family holding me as a newborn made me realise how loved I was.

I continued to flip through the photo album, taking the time to examine every image closely in how it formed part of my wider story.

An hour later, I closed the photo album.

My eyes closed.

I breathed a heavy sigh of relief.

I looked up to the sky and smiled.

I was one of the lucky ones.

My birth was the beginning.

It taught me early – I fight.

All those setbacks and all the tough times have led me to this moment.

The moment I stand here and recount the story I have been building over the past twenty-three years.

My life was shaped by circumstances I didn't choose and decisions I had to make. I can't sit here and tell you that every single choice I have made has worked. That's what growing up is, it's learning, changing, and striving towards what we see as our ideal future.

This story doesn't pretend everything works out perfectly. It's not a tale of how pain doesn't hurt and how words don't scar. I've felt both. But that pain passes, and if you allow it, it can strengthen you, rather than shrink you.

In the chapters that follow, I will share moments that tested my confidence and that challenged who I was becoming. Not because I have all the answers, but because I learned which questions I needed to ask.

This is where my story begins.

For the first time, I'm ready to tell it.

CHAPTER TWO
REFLECTIONS FROM THE DINING TABLE

'You know we're here for you no matter what, right?'

'Right.' I nodded.

Our dinner table was where the tough days made sense again. The four of us sharing those quiet dinners became some of my most cherished moments.

Such situations were regular in our house. Ava, Mum, Dad and I would always meet at the table to discuss the ups and downs of each of our days. Mum and Dad would tell the latest anecdotes from their burgeoning careers while Ava would often tell stories about what she did at school or dancing. I also took great pride in my happenings and friendships built at school.

Even before Ava and I were big enough to sit at the grown-up dining table, we would often share a small kid-friendly table adorned with blue colouring and sea creatures, often chomping down on delicious meals while watching a mix of the news or children's programming.

Whenever I needed their support and guidance, they would help me with the utmost confidence. From a very young age, that is what the Robertson way was to me, to be caring to others, and to never be afraid to have fun.

One of my favourite memories is from about age nine or ten. As a child growing up in a world that was becoming increasingly glued to technology, I sometimes struggled with the concept of going outside to play. In my mind, I would have much rathered conquer another evil videogame king as Super Mario.

One afternoon, my parents put away our screens and instructed us to go outside for an hour. My sister was compliant, but I was hesitant.

Mum and Dad sat on the front step of our house and set a timer for one hour. For the life of me, I have no idea why they didn't just get up and go inside. They sat on that step for the entire hour, watching and laughing as Ava and I rode our bikes up our paved driveway.

Ava and I would try to race each other up and down the driveway, seeing who could ride up the steep pavement and back in record time. The true test came in trying to constantly race each other and remembering to brake before the deck and its tiling.

As well as our bike races, I would throw a tennis ball against the wall, desperately trying to catch it with an outstretched arm before it zinged against the floor and over the fence.

Other memories bring similar comfort. Times such as when we would be swimming around in our pool and playing games of volleyball against one another. There were all those nights we would camp out on the couch watching movies where I would obliterate bowls of popcorn. The times we walked our dog Harry around Light Street Park also bring back many memories of the great outdoors.

However, the one thing that still connects us all are those moments of joy we created together for many, many years.

My family has two distinct sides and two very distinct stories. My father was born in Dalwallinu, a small country town nearly 300 kilometres from Perth. He always beamed with pride retelling his experiences as a country boy, including his successful outings in county cricket. Without fail, every time we passed certain venues, he would spout the tales of when he hit opposing bowlers for six.

My mother's side of the family is also incredibly rich with history. Mum was born in Perth, but her lineage goes much further than that. Both of my maternal grandparents are Italian, making their way to Perth at very young ages. Mum always told us growing up of her excitement at special events and celebrations with her Italian relatives.

Growing up in a family such as this made me feel deeply connected to my cultural heritage. I always loved telling other kids at school of my Dad's connections to country WA, or the exciting anecdotes from my mother's deep Italian heritage. My family taught me the value of respecting your roots. It can be very easy to feel lost as you become your own person, I grew up in an environment where I was told from day one that where I came from held great value.

They inspire me to become someone I am proud of. They always give me unconditional support and guidance. This extends not only from my immediate family, but to my extended relatives and other close friends. I am incredibly proud that my family has seen its fair share of new additions, people who were not born into our tribe but who make it even more special. From stepparents to partners, even a little stepsister, I am incredibly grateful that new people have been brought into my life and have taught me countless lessons.

Then there's my ever-conquering sidekick, Ava. As a little sister, she has taught me so much about believing in myself and not giving a flying f what anyone else thinks. I have never, ever met someone with the confidence of a thirty-something year old at the age of six.

One of my fondest memories with Ava is growing up where we would create our own television show on our trampoline (this is when I knew she belonged on the stage). There were the times we would camp out in the loungeroom together and watch movies. But my favourite memory we've shared was in 2021, the day we first met our stepsister Amelia shortly after her birth.

I lean on my family in tough times. They are my sounding board, the voices in my head to tell me where I need to put myself. Most importantly of all, they do not sugarcoat. They tell me things straight, they never fail to keep me humble and honest with myself. That is the greatest gift of all.

Family are the people we didn't choose, but who choose us anyways. I have always taken great pride in my family. The fact I get to call myself a Robertson makes me incredibly proud. Family are the people who remind us who we were before the world told us who to become. They appear in the everyday moments, present or unseen. Their presence reminds us that we can face whatever comes our way.

I have always taken great pride in my family. The fact I get to call myself a Robertson (as well as a number of other last names) makes me incredibly proud. Family are the people who remind us who we were before the world told us who to become. They appear in the everyday moments, present or unseen. Their presence reminds us that we can face whatever comes our way.

It is only when we lean on our family, that we can achieve true strength, and even greater compassion within ourselves.

I didn't choose my family.

But they chose me – on hard days, on the quiet nights, on the afternoons that didn't feel important at the time.

Looking back, those moments were bigger than I knew.

I'll remember most not the big milestones.

Just our dinner table.

The steep driveway.

The noise.

The cheer.

My biggest supporters.

I DIDN'T RIDE TODAY

I remember it like it was yesterday.
Rolling down a steep hill.
Feet pedaling faster than I thought possible.
The wind in my face.
'I'm going to make it!'
Then I lost control.
The handlebars shook beneath me.
I swerved.
Left. Right.
My knee hit the pavement.
I remember the silence after.
My Dad walked over, calm as ever.
'It'll be okay, Tom, you're just a little banged up.'
I knew he was right.
But I didn't ride again.
Not the next day.
Not the next week.
I told myself I was through.
Until one afternoon, my parents packed the car and drove me
to Light Street.
I didn't want to be there.
But I got on the bike anyway.
I got on the seat, feet in place.
I fixed my eyes on the path ahead.
Pedals began to turn.
One rotation.
Then another.
'I'm doing it!'
I glanced back.
No hands.
They had let go.
My heartbeat quickened.
I wasn't ready.
But I didn't stop.
I narrowed my eyes and quickly steered left.
And once more.
I was riding, actually riding.
I kept going. Faster now, steadier.
No help, no hands. Just me.
Falling wasn't what stopped me. Staying down was.

CHAPTER THREE
YOU CAN'T PLEASE EVERYONE

I used to sit at the top of the climbing frame at our school playground.

I would peer over the edge at the sandpit and other colourful play equipment. I felt like the king of the world.

With all my might, I let go of the frame, jumping forward and throwing my body in the air like a contortionist. I landed knees first into the pit below. I sat up, shook the many grains of sand off my grey and blue uniform, and climbed again.

'Thomas, why are you jumping off the climbing frame?'

'Because it's fun! I'm trying to see if I can land on my feet.'

When I wasn't scaling structures and pretending to be an Olympic level jumper, I would often spend Recess and Lunchtimes playing soccer at the oval opposite our school with the other boys, pretending we were vying for the World Cup. We would also play footy, handball, and often enjoyed the game of tag or two.

I really enjoyed my time there. It was a large school catering to students from Kindy all the way to Year 6, as is common in most Australian schools. The teachers genuinely cared about us students, I made some of my most treasured friendships at school, and the sense of community could be felt from classrooms to playdates.

The main reason I loved my first school was that they gave me a chance. I was born with tight calf muscles and as a result, this affected the way I walked. I was required to wear splints and casts on my legs throughout my initial years of schooling. I felt heavily supported in my journey.

My first introduction to social interaction and friendship largely came through my cousins. I always enjoyed going to sporting events, sharing trips and simply catching up with them. Coming from a large family myself, I came to appreciate the care and unconditional support they gave me on my journey.

I learned to form positive relationships as a kid through trial and error. I was a very shy boy, which meant making friends was quite hard for me. I usually liked to go about things and not make much of a fuss, but I didn't realise at the time that being shy was actively preventing myself from meeting new people.

So naturally, I began to get curious.

At six, while on the edge of the sandpit, observing the other children playing, I decided to take a chance and meet some new people. I nervously walked up to a group of boys playing football and asked if I could join. They looked me up and down and said 'Sorry, our game is already full.'

'Oh, sorry.' I said, turning to walk away.

'But, we could always use one more player, we're playing King of the Pack.'

I then ran over to the game and attempted to mark the ball, desperately trying not to scrape my legs on the hot basketball court.

We ended up playing for the whole of Recess together.

The next day, we played footy again.

And many days after.

As was natural with school, friendships would of course change over time. I often connected more with the boys in my classes due to their various interests in sport, computer games and wrestling. I wouldn't say I initially had a group of friends set in stone but was happy to be a floater and get to know different people. The most pivotal of those friendships, however, was with a girl.

She was one of the kindest people I had ever met, her excitement, her bubbly nature and her genuine care for others made her an ideal sidekick for my misadventures. She was naturally athletic and a popular friendly face in our cohort. We would often chase our friends around the school in competitive games of chasey, as well as often make up songs and dances. It's been over a decade since we last saw each other, but those many memories we made as children will stay with me for a long time. I realised why hanging out with her made me so happy, because she truly made me feel seen, and I could tell that the time we spent meant a lot to her too. We would regularly go on playdates at each other's houses and always stick by each other in times of trouble.

The ways she would tell ridiculous jokes and burst out laughing, the ways we would come up with new character names for people. It always puts a smile on my face to reminisce the fun we had.

She taught me what having a best friend really meant.

And I'll always remember that.

My experiences of forming friendships were not all perfect, but they were human. I knew that not everyone liked me or got me, and it bothered me. Comments would be made from other boys about the way I walked or the casts I would wear, I tried not to let it faze me.

But you could only try so much.

I learned that not everyone really understood who Thomas was, and I was setting myself up for failure by expecting everyone would.

But that's life, right?

As I went through later years, I began to become more comfortable in myself. Not through some divine intervention or magic moment where my fortunes changed, instead through making mistakes.

During lessons, I would sometimes act eccentric or try to be louder than usual to get the attention of people. I wanted to be noticed, to make friends. But my classmates found this behaviour particularly annoying and told my teacher as a result. In Year 2 this became a particular problem. I would often keep poking and prodding at classmates to get the attention of popular boys in our class. One of the boys got very upset at me and told the teacher about my continued antagonising. As a result, I walked with a duty teacher at Lunch.

Despite me not being sure in who I was, my teachers made every effort and then some to make me feel included. When they saw I was lonely at Recess or Lunchtimes, they would often ask me what was wrong and find me a buddy to play with. It was those same teachers that would inspire me to one day follow in their footsteps.

In Year 3, I was taught by Mr. Cavanaugh, my first of two male teachers in primary school. He became a favourite of mine and was always willing to lend a hand when I was in need of help. But the biggest impact he had on me wasn't the teaching of content, instead in the things he said. One day I was acting particularly frustrated and began to tease and mock some of the girls in our class. I was upset that I had no one to play with and decided to take my feelings out on my classmates.

As I was sitting on the floor near the doorway, Mr. Cavanaugh came over to me and asked what was wrong.

'I don't have anyone to play with. I feel lonely.'

'Thomas, the way you're feeling is perfectly normal. But I know for a fact there are plenty of people in this class that would love to play with you.'

'All you have to do is ask. It can be scary but otherwise people won't know you want to play with them.'

'How else will people know you want to play if you don't tell them?'

He was right.

So, my usual friends and I played soccer at Recess. My problem wasn't that I wasn't liked, it was that I wouldn't let myself establish those connections. I became too shy and scared of being told no that I kept myself away and wanted attention to come to me.

I then sought to make meaningful connections that made me happy. I knew that positive friendships came from shared interests and acceptance of others. As a result of my patience and proactive approach to friendships, I remained close with the same group of friends in both Year 4 and 5.

December 2013 marked my last day at my first school. I was due to move to a school near the city for Year 6 and high school. That day was a memory that I will never forget.

The whole class had gifted me a signed basketball and we had a class party to celebrate the last day of school. My school faction shirt was signed by both Year 5 classes. I remember my last hug with my best friend being particularly tearful as we didn't know when we would see each other again.

Leaving schools was hard, but accepting the change was harder.

Those school holidays I had to say goodbye to a part of me that had shaped the boy I was. But, I knew change was on the horizon.

With change however came great uncertainty.

I was set to move to a new school, the same that my cousins

Mason, Jordan and Liam would all attend at some point. I knew virtually nothing about the school and was even more surprised when I was accepted in.

Soon, came a swift transition from navy and grey to blue and green. I was a new man now.

My parents and I had been analysing every single email or letter sent out to us as the new school year began, scouring the class list to make some sense of the faces I would be joining next year.

It was a delight though when I found out that I would have a male teacher in Year 6, especially since Mr. Cavanaugh had such a major impact on me. However, the night before my impending transition, I began to panic.

I couldn't shake this feeling of dread.

Would the other boys like me?

Would I live up to the high standards the school holds?

Would I be able to make the same meaningful connections I did at my old school?

As I drifted to sleep that night, I came to a painful albeit vital truth. Friends come and go from our lives.

The people that are meant to be will stay. It sounds like an easy thing to say, but you will be amazed how many relationships you will endure throughout your life. Those friends that accept you, not who approve of you, are the ones that will stay. You will lose friends and gain new friends, that is all a part of growing up.

Always be sure to give yourself credit for being able to put your best foot forward in that friendship or relationship. The heartbreak may hurt or even sting for a while, but there will be the right people for you.

In time, I was able to move on and figure out what exactly I wanted out of the right people for me. I could take a step back and consider the traits or interests I would want a true friend to have.

I spent a long time trying to be liked by everyone.

It never worked.

The more I tried, the further away I felt from myself.

The friendships that lasted weren't the ones I forced.

They were the ones where I didn't have to change anything at all.

I was ready to step through new gates and meet new faces.

I soon learned that you can't please everyone.

CHAPTER FOUR
THE PUZZLE I COULDN'T SOLVE

As I walked through the gates of my new school for the first time, the weight of expectation was heavily on my mind.

I scanned around the school grounds, seeing boys playing handball, the same grey buttoned shirts and dark shorts permeating the entire campus.

The uniforms felt different.

The expectations felt lofty.

I was the same.

As I was confronted with the rambunctious noise and ringing of the bell, I lowered my head and nervously walked up the steps, avoiding eye contact with anyone who dare looked my way.

My parents walked with me to Year 6 Green, my now classroom. We were greeted by my teacher, Mr. Hayes. He looked down at me with a beaming smile and outstretched his hand to shake mine. He then guided me into our classroom where I would meet my brothers in arms.

As I stepped through the classroom, I was greeted with a smattering of looks. Some boys smiled back at me, others didn't take as much interest. I soon sat at my desk next to a few of the other boys in my class. They each introduced themselves before turning their attention to me and my past.

'So where have you come from Tom?'

Didn't realise we were going straight to nicknames.

'My last school was in Tuart Hill, I really liked it there.'

'Oh nice! We've been here since Year 4.'

Our school did not start at Kindy, they began taking kids on from Year 4, through to Year 12.

I very quickly tried to make sense of my new life. On our first day at school, we did swimming trials in the school pool. This was something I didn't really mind but found foreign. At my old school we would catch a bus to a local aquatic centre and do our lessons and carnival there. Our campus had its own pool, this was a welcome change of pace.

Being here meant being part of a team.

By joining the blue and green brigade, you were hereby encouraged to be a role model for others, to preach the school's values. This was especially true in the social aspect of school. At lunchtimes I would regularly play soccer with some of the other boys on the school oval, just as I would at my old school.

One thing became very apparent each day, these boys weren't playing for fun. They were playing to be the best.

Every pass brought a weight of competitiveness; each shot at goal screamed desperation. These boys wanted to be the best and that same drive appeared in their schoolwork. My classmates prided themselves on achieving great results, whether this be in Literacy or Maths or specialist subjects including Art or Music.

My journey to forming friendships largely came through making myself uncomfortable. I knew I couldn't hide behind my fear forever.

I was first introduced to friends through common circumstance. We were put into houses or factions. I was in the red and blue faction. It was through class and sporting endeavours that I met one of my best friends.

He had come from a school in the northern suburbs like me, his family lived near the beach. He was a keen footy player and volleyballer, a natural athlete if there ever was one.

We became close friends largely due to this being our first year. We soon also managed to build our relationship on our shared love for basketball and the West Coast Eagles. Our times hanging out and competing in videogames was always a highlight.

As well as this, I also began to make friends with two other boys. Largely, we all shared a common interest in soccer and were keen FIFA players. They had both been at the school since Year 4 and were both incredible athletes. They loved their sport and both played competitive soccer outside of school.

I soon through these three boys and many others began to find my feet at school. Through finding safe space in our Recess and Lunchtime shenanigans, I felt like I was part of the fabric.

Almost.

Soon boys became fixated on the way I acted.

When I would laugh at someone's joke or ask to join a game, they would approach with some hesitancy.

The reason? Tenure.

Some, not all, boys felt that because I was a new player they knew better and were wary about me stepping into their world, their friendships, their passions.

It hit me, these boys didn't like me because I wasn't sure enough in myself. I let them talk down to me and used their words as reasons to lose sight of who I was.

One Recess, I wanted to try my hand at playing football with a group of boys. I had never really played football that much but loved the sport. One of the boys kicked a long bomb out from the goal square, I ran over to mark it, but the ball slipped through my hands.

The boy rolled his eyes.

'Hey! Why didn't you mark that?'

'I tried, I'm sorry…'

I turned to walk away.

Another Lunch break, I was scolded for being too nice. We were playing a game of soccer and things got quite competitive, I was jostling for the ball with another student. They swiped the ball from my legs and took a shot, sailing just wide of the goal.

'Why are you even playing with us? All you'll do is be a teacher's pet, you're a terrible soccer player.'

'You're too nice.'

Eager not to let this boy's words get to me, I collected the ball before dribbling through an onslaught of outstretched legs, slotting the ball past the keeper.

I turned to the boy, shrugging my shoulders as I leapt in the air celebrating.

I could tell he regretted his prior comment.

As the bell rang to head back to class, the other boy saw the smile on my face and approached me.

'You know what Tom? I'm sorry, there's never such a thing as being too nice.'

We shook hands before walking back to class.

As I rode home that day it hit me, maybe I was too nice. Maybe I was too innocent or too shy for this school.

Was it possible I was an outsider?

Were the other boys right?

I had lost my grip on who I was.

I thought being at this school meant embracing your gifts, harnessing your special qualities.

Maybe, I was wrong.

The version of me I sought to become was one that fit in line with my place of education. Yes, it was great that I had made more friends and begun to really enjoy schooling life, but I didn't really know or care who I was outside of that. Weekends and quiet hours were spent talking to school friends or doing activities I would normally associate with school, such as sporting practice.

I had become a part of a team but lost who I was in the process.

We are all dressed up in the same uniform, attending the same classes, learning the same material. While I deeply value the power of education as a safe space, I remember feeling this overwhelming sense of wanting to be different. Being surrounded by peers and friends made me feel like another number, another student passing through the halls. That's where my sense of personal identity struggled to take shape. There was pressure to fit in with my friend group, pressure to achieve grades I felt were strong, pressure to keep my self-designated 'clean-cut private school boy' image.

So, I sought to just be myself.

I came to a realisation that who I was would not appear overnight. It was through a practice of trial and error that I would find the things that made me the most unique.

I just had to stay true to myself.

It was through my first year at my new school that I learned that there was no expectation on me.

I was creating the narrative.

How I would fare would ultimately be a result of my own actions and decisions.

By taking risks and actively seeking new opportunities in Year 6, I was able to gain a greater understanding of the kind of person I wanted to be.

As a result, more friendships and connections flourished.

Finding your people does not happen when you are comfortable. It happens when you stop chasing access, stop over-explaining yourself, and stop tearing apart your boundaries just to stay welcome. It happens when you are willing to sit with loneliness and those quiet nights instead of simply settling for connection that costs you self-esteem.

The people meant for you won't require you to shrink or change. They won't need constant approval-seeking to keep them close by. They will meet you where you are and not where they expect you to be.

For years, I thought standing out meant being extraordinary. Turns out it meant being authentic.

One year later, as I packed my school bag ready for the first day of high school, I realised something.

The team was the same.

People would change.

Who I am was just beginning to take shape.

I was ready to continue the search.

Not for attention, but for acceptance.

I didn't know where it would take me, but I knew that I was strong enough to try.

CHAPTER FIVE
CHOOSING YOUR CIRCLE

High school was never meant to be straightforward.

I still remember my first day of Year 7.

Walking into the giant undercover courtyard, seeing 120 odd other teenage boys dressed in our summer uniforms, was a surreal experience. We were all there to form positive social relationships and achieve the best we could academically.

My appearance in high school was slightly different to how I appear now. I was about 5 foot 5, I certainly weighed a bit less than I do now. I used to always slick my hair back with an ungodly amount of gel and had sheepishly skinny arms and legs. So, naturally, I felt a bit self-conscious and pressured to fit in with the 'cool kids' in my year group.

With high school came a faster schedule, more pressure, more hierarchy, a louder environment. Everything got drastically more serious almost overnight. I wasn't prepared for the curveballs that would be soon thrown my way.

Individual timetables, lockers, sport on a Thursday afternoon. These were all changes that took me a bit of time getting used to, to be honest the canteen food helped.

I had carried over several friends from Junior School, who were there to excitedly greet me on day one of our high school journey. We were in awe of the multiple story buildings housing classrooms and wide-open spaces. We couldn't believe we were finally in high school.

It was a lot for my twelve-year-old self to take in.

But I wouldn't have much time to stop and smell the roses. Before I knew it, we were on the clock.

I was soon hauled into my Year 7 English class after a brief orientation seminar from several teachers. It was through icebreakers and sheer force from the staff that I soon met several of my soon to be friends. They were all like-minded boys arriving from a smattering of other schools across Perth.

I didn't know it at the time, but these people would shape the next six years of my life in ways I could never expect. Soon, I formed a core friendship group with some other boys. In various pairings and groups, we would regularly meet up before school to play handball and run around madly at break times on the oval playing soccer.

It felt nice to meet some boys who valued me for me, and with whom I could genuinely connect with. It wasn't their company I appreciated the most, but the fact they accepted me without judgement.

I would regularly spend time at their houses on playdates, and we often bonded over our love of sport, videogames and general online meme culture. I felt I could be myself around them. It was refreshing. At least at first.

As my body developed and I grew older, I began to become more wary of the boys I had dedicated so much of my time to. Not because of any dislike or mistrust, but because of their own social expansions. They slowly began to make friends with many other students. I felt our connections slipping away.

This threat of losing my friends instantly caused me to spiral. I began to become more jealous, more irritated towards them. They had not done anything wrong. They were just merely branching out, like every young person does.

I just wouldn't let myself accept it.

In Year 8 and 9, I too found peace in other people.

I began to engage more with boys involved in the school's music program, as I was a member of choir and took piano lessons at school.

My problem didn't lie with my friends finding new ones, it lay in my unwillingness to be forgotten quickly. Around those boys I began to feel unnerving emotions, I felt awkward, stressed and unhappy. I would avoid them and try to distance myself from them. What I failed to realise was by outwardly displaying my jealousy, I pushed them away.

I didn't want to be replaced.

Yet, I didn't consider this may have not been the case.

I struggled to cope with my friends finding other friends because maybe I wasn't so certain in my loyalty to them in the first place.

I got on with my friends reasonably well, we would often do things outside of school and regularly spend time together while in class. There was no real issue of chemistry or connection.

I just wasn't sure in what kind of friend I was to them.

So, I had a decision to make.

Would I chase approval and put myself at risk of coming across too keen?

Or would I test the waters with other friendships and try to expand my connections?

I began to sit next to different people in classes, wanting to learn more about some of my peers who I maybe hadn't paid as much focus to in prior years. On the bus rides to and from sport, I would make a point of sitting in a different spot every time, to talk to someone new.

From this uncomfortable exercise came a chance to make new friendships and learn more about some of the other boys I went to school with.

This approach seemed to be working well.

I strolled into Year 10 with a strong sense of confidence in myself and greater social awareness.

That was until fate decided to remind me of the other friends I had neglected in branching out.

One day my Nonna and I were driving down Beaufort Street to go to the city. As we were stopped at a traffic light, I noticed something out the window.

At a bus stop stood the boys I had given so much of my time too.

Why wasn't I there?

I told my Nonna and she saw them standing there talking gleefully. She sympathised with me as we then decided to go home.

I was in a world of hurt when I walked through the front door,

I couldn't believe what I had just seen.

Me and the boys had a good run.

Maybe this was the not so swift conclusion?

I tried to tell myself not to think much of it.

To be strong.

But I just couldn't do it.

I approached one of the boys at the school library the next

day, expressing my disappointment at not being invited to their outing.

As he tried to search for a way to excuse himself of blame, one part of our chat struck me more than any other.

'We're not your people.'

'You'll find your people at university, that's where everyone finds their people.'

'We're friends, of course we are, but we're not your people.'

I took a step back, admittedly stunned.

But deep down, he was right.

I couldn't run away from the truth, we just weren't meant for each other. At least not in that timeframe.

As much as I loved those boys, something just wasn't clicking with me in that friend group. I got resentful and let my jealousy cloud my true feelings towards my friend group.

I was alone.

Or so my mind would tell me.

Grappling with this surprise that I saw coming from a mile away, I sought to find solace in my other friends.

After all, in a school of over one hundred young men, there had to be some other people I could interact with. So, I threw myself into making myself uncomfortable.

I began to visit the library before school and in breaktimes, playing cricket on the oval rather than soccer. It felt good, it felt nice to branch out and interact with other people.

If there is one thing growing up has taught me, it's that acceptance matters more than approval, and that the path towards it is rarely ever comfortable.

Approval demands performance and action. It asks you to bend, to change yourself just enough to be deemed useful. Acceptance however is quiet, it doesn't need constant reassurance and positive feedback. It doesn't ask you to jump through hoops. It exists without limits or barriers.

Coming out of my shell socially allowed me to form a clearer picture of who I am. Looking back, my self-doubt actively charged me forward to learn about my identity and how I see myself.

But something was missing.

The banter.

The camaraderie.

The inside jokes.

I looked over to the boys and thought to myself that there must be some reason we clicked so well all these years. Even if we weren't in each other's pockets or around each other every moment of each day, we still were friends.

Friends fight, friends have disagreements.

Just because we didn't connect on every level didn't mean they were worth dropping in a hurry. I had to be a bigger man and accept that I could in fact have multiple friend groups.

I knew that my friends would change in high school.

It would never be a constant six years.

There were great days of connection and happiness.

Other days were ones of tension and envy.

I was still figuring myself out.

And I didn't have to chase anymore.

CHAPTER SIX
BETWEEN THE WHITE LINES

I always wanted to score a goal in a soccer game.

The pure feeling of elation, the excitement to know you had just added to your team's total. That is what I was chasing. I couldn't stop thinking about how special it would be to make my scoring mark in a game. After all, I had played the FIFA videogames for years, how hard could it be to repeat the trick in real life?

I anxiously looked over my shoulder for signs of a defender as my legs pushed me down the left wing. My eyes scanned the pitch for a teammate to feed. With all the force my left foot could muster, I sent the ball down the middle before charging down the left side of the pitch, desperate to get in on the action.

'Yes, ball!!!!' I yelled.

As I emerged in front of my opponent, the ball stretched out in front of me, I scrambled to meet it. I looked up to see the goalkeeper staring me down, I was all alone in the box.

This was the moment.

I met the keeper with a steely eyed gaze, shifted my body weight, and stuck the ball with the outside of my right boot.

I saw the ball roll at great speed. It kept travelling, closer and closer. The goalkeeper remained planted still.

My whole body waited in anticipation, even for a split second.

The ball rolled between the keeper's legs and ended up in the back of the net. I wheeled away in celebration, sticking my arms out to mimic the wings of an airplane.

That was my first goal.

I never chased that feeling again. I chased what it gave me.

Sport was everywhere growing up. From watching many cousins try their hand at soccer, to regularly watching cricket with my Dad at lunchtimes, it has always provided me with an exhilaration like no other.

I had first properly tried my hand at sport playing soccer as a child, for clubs in our local area. Sport didn't just mean turning up for the team. It meant turning up for myself – something I wasn't always good at.

The biggest gain from playing sport as a child was that it also provided me with freedom to be myself, a journey that I would embark on mainly through high school.

Fortunately, I was at school that prided its sport program as part of its extra-curricular lifestyle. We would play against other private schools who found their home in the Perth metro area. As part of playing sport, we had to select both a Summer and a Winter sport. Choosing soccer for my winter sport was a no brainer, I had fallen in love with the game as a child and wanted to enjoy that same experience with my mates. My choice of summer sport however was a little bit trickier.

In the end, I settled on basketball. Most of my friends were playing the sport and I had a relatively large love of the NBA and my Miami Heat, so it seemed a great fit.

My initial years playing basketball at school helped me gain more confidence in myself. I had never really played the sport before, but what made it the most special was the fact I got to play with my mates. I didn't score many baskets, but I tried to always encourage my teammates where necessary. I treated basketball as a secondary, backseat endeavour to my soccer pursuits. I loved the sport sure, but it was not my main area of focus.

Soccer season was where I really sunk my teeth into school sport.

As was the nature of our school and cohort, it became quite competitive for places in the school's A and B teams. Initially I took this quite personally but soon realised that I would be happier playing at a level where I could just enjoy myself. Playing soccer also helped me achieve one beautiful goal, it helped me grow a lot closer to boys I hadn't really hung around in a school setting.

Gradually over Year 7 and 8, we would always love heading out to interschool sport on Thursday afternoons. Our games were also a personal highlight. As a C team we performed decently, winning more games than lost. We would regularly discuss tactics and come up with new ways to get under our opponents' skins. This level of friendship and trust led to some big wins over our rival schools.

But my favourite sporting experience did not happen within school gates, rather because of them. My older cousin worked at a local indoor sports centre not far from home. This gave me the idea to form an indoor soccer team with my mates at school. So, I rounded up eight of the best and we formed Fake Madrid, a team name with very similar ties to one of the world's greatest sporting franchises.

Before too long, the wins piled up. We had won over hearts and our own minds with our brand of unique and slightly unorthodox football. Often, this would be a case of hoofing the ball over the tops of defenders to whomever would be running down the wings. More often than not, it worked a treat.

Before too long, we had momentum on our side. We were eventually scheduled to face a team made of other boys from our school cohort. Right before this game I called us boys into a huddle. I then proceeded to give a pre-match rev-up speech full of words I am not willing to repeat here. We eventually came out winners.

The following season, our bond on and off the pitch seemed to work wonders as we made it to the grand final, beating our school foes to get there with two goals that had to be seen to be believed. Through sheer grit, some fierce tackling and some luck, we managed to drag the game out to penalties, where my teammates managed to absolutely bury all five into the back of the net.

We had become indoor champions.

Even though my friends so hilariously pointed out to me that we were playing against kids a year younger than us, I was still rapt with the achievement. It was through this moment of winning the title that I realised why I loved playing soccer so much, the small wins. Those small moments of joy that you share with your teammates and friends are what made sport so special to me.

My enjoyment of indoor soccer naturally made my passion for sport grow. It was during this time that I began to practice my skills more at the park as well as watching more YouTube tutorials on how to complete certain maneuvers on the pitch to evade defenders. With this renewed energy, I was ready to approach the interschool season with excitement and joy.

But, in Year 10, things changed.

It stopped being fun.

Feeling quite bothered by the seriousness of school sport, I began taking my anger and frustration out on other people. I overhit passes and brashly stormed in for tackles, throwing my whole body at opposing players. The love for the game I once had slipped because I took myself far too seriously.

In Year 11, I had made the 4ths soccer team, which meant I would be playing in a somewhat worse division than years prior. I was heavily determined to change my attitude about sport and get back to making it an enjoyable experience.

This would also be the year I scored a rare goal that I was pretty proud of. Against a rival school, we were playing against a bunch of Year 12's. Although we were a weaker team on paper, we still put in 110% on the field. We had gone down 3-0 at halftime and things were looking pretty bleak.

The second half whistle blew.

They scored their fourth.

Then, their fifth.

I was absolutely downtrodden.

Not long after, one of my teammates strode forward with the ball, bearing down on goal. He was brought down by a vicious tackle on the edge of the box. A free kick was awarded.

I sheepishly stepped up to the plate, anxious to take the set piece.

I had never taken a free kick in a real game before.

I tensed my body and took a deep breath in.

One foot came forward, then quicker steps.

I struck the ball with the inside of my right boot.

The ball began its orbit, curling around the wall of three defenders, and past the goalkeeper for our only goal of the game.

I was ecstatic.

My teammates mobbed me as I jogged back to the centre circle. I had just scored the kind of goal you dream about as a boy watching the best in the world. My friends hi-fived me and patted me on the back, giving compliments and genuine looks of shock. I felt happy with myself for scoring, but even happier for how my friends encouraged me.

I had found my reason for playing.

It was never scoring goals.

It was them.

The day after, our Science teacher (who was also our coach at the time) very affectionately referred to me as 'Bend it Like Beckham.' I took a great liking to that name, laughing at it in jest.

As the year went on, I began to take less of a serious approach to my sporting endeavours and decided to just have fun with it. I would turn up to training cracking jokes with friends, losing the former ritual of listening to music and zoning out all else. I had once again found joy in the sport that had first opened its doors to me as a child. I was no longer concerned with being the best, I was concerned whether I was truly having fun.

Year 12 came along and I was promoted to 3rds Soccer. I was excited about playing in a new team and at a slightly higher level. We had a successful season and I was finding my footing playing on the right wing. I was never the quickest or the most agile, but I like to think my strength lay in my vision on the pitch, and my ability to judge where to pass the ball and what runs to make.

Soon came our last match of the season and our last ever interschool encounter. Funnily enough, the team I scored THAT free-kick against were our opponent that day. My family and I arrived at the expansive and green playing fields, and I was determined to have an enjoyable last hit out.

While training before the match, I looked over at the 4ths team, seeing many of my mates that I had grown up playing with. I wondered if maybe we could have one last joy on the pitch together before we graduated.

Never a better time like the present.

I politely asked my coach if I could play with the 4ths for our final game as I wanted to be with my friends. He looked at me with some confusion but granted my request.

The band was back together.

That game was like no other I ever played, the energy we had as a team was electric. Knowing it was our last ever sporting contest for our school, we pulled out all the stops. Passes were being played all over the field, we were thumping shots at the goal. We just couldn't find a way in.

The other boys made sure to capitalise on that.

Due to defensive errors and a lack of athletic prowess to catch up with opposing attackers, our opponents put four past us before halftime.

Soon, the whistle blew.

I trudged back to our team huddle, crestfallen.

I wasn't in the mood for talking, I was frustrated that this was our last time together. We were losing 4-0 despite having countless chances and shots at our disposal. But I knew we had to carry on. So, I slowly picked myself up off the ground and called my teammates over.

We linked arms and I delivered my second ever speech for such an occasion. It was five words long.

'Boys, let's just score one.'

We all chanted and danced around, ready to come out fighting in the second half.

We kept the score the same for thirty of the forty minutes of that half, our resolve proving tough for the defence to break down. I thought I would be responsible for their fifth goal, when a long ball flew over my head and towards our goalkeeper. I chased down the opposing attacker, narrowly collecting the ball before their outstretched leg could trip me up. I rolled the ball behind me with my heel, swiftly losing my defender.

I then belted the ball up the field before bursting up the pitch to reach the edge of our attacking box. I looked over at the ball coming towards me airborne. My right foot rose to strike it on the volley, my body shifting around to meet it. The ball sailed towards the goal, narrowly scraping the right post.

So, so close.

Despite our fighting spirit, we unfortunately went on to lose that game 7-0, conceding three goals in the last ten minutes owing to defensive blunders and accuracy on our opponent's part. While it was not the ideal way to bow out of school sport, it was a morning that I will never forget. Not for the end result, but for the joy of playing the game I love with people I love one last time.

As I walked across the graduation stage weeks later, I was reminded of all the battles. Those tough tussles on the pitch and the trying academic rigour off it. The friendship squabbles that turned into moments of embrace and support. I could say with full confidence that during my high school experience, I truly left it all out there on the field.

Over the course of my life, sport has always been a constant.
Sport built my confidence.
Then took it away.
Somewhere in between, I found out who I was when playing.

CHAPTER SEVEN
THE MIRROR ISN'T THE TRUTH

When walking into my first university class, I felt I didn't belong.

I was met with a sea of new faces and names to remember. These people by appearance alone looked like they had things all together. My insecurity senses tingled furiously as we were asked to convene in a circle in one of many convenient icebreakers.

Being a male studying in a female dominated field of primary teaching presented its own unique set of challenges for me. It forced me to rethink how I saw myself – and how I thought other people saw me.

I began to meet more people in those initial weeks of our course. Gradually those first connections formed into blossoming friendships with people from all walks of life here to convene with a shared goal of changing the world.

Over the coming weeks, I would make friends with several people I am still close with to this day. I slowly began to come more out of my shell through ice-breaker activities and by simple small talk. It felt like I had found my place at university and was optimistic about my ability to form new relationships.

But then, something happened.

It was in Week 3 or 4 where I started to have major bouts of anxiety about my place within my university cohort. Suddenly, I became more intimidated by the ever-expanding groups of boys that strolled into classes talking about what they did on the weekend. I began to feel threatened and anxious about the many girls that would also form similar cliques. I felt out of place.

I grew to form a close friend group of other boys around my age. We'd regularly discuss our favourite music, share memes on Instagram, and discuss some of their more social adventures over each weekend. However, despite this acceptance, something still felt off.

My mornings at university went from brightly walking into classrooms and auditoriums to slowly trailing behind others, keeping my head low. I was desperate not to be noticed by my peers, my frame and stature became pressures for me. Suddenly, I began wearing baggier clothes, paid less attention to the way I dressed. Outside I fronted a calm exterior, inside I slowly questioned my armor I begrudgingly donned to classes each day.

One afternoon, I caught the bus home, pulling my hoodie tightly over my face in a desperate attempt to go unbothered. No music played in my earphones, but my glances out the window spoke volumes. As I took in the sights of buildings, shopping centres, passing pedestrians, a question formed into my head.

'What makes those things so beautiful and deservedly noticed?'

My eyes began to well up as I tagged off the bus and sprinted home. I didn't feel in control of myself.

I burst through the front door, almost slamming it behind me, my black laptop bag flying across the hallway. Bedsheets were furiously ripped over my body as I began to sob uncontrollably at the sight of my physical condition. I was losing grip on myself, and I didn't like it. I tossed and turned before getting to sleep much earlier than necessary.

'I can't bear to look at myself.' I muttered.

Why was I so harsh on my body and psyche?

I suppose the fact I was born premature has always lended feelings of being different. At 17, comparison continued to rear its ugly head. When starting university, I had only just left high school, with very limited life experience. But, that didn't need to be a bad thing.

One Sunday evening, I clearly remember looking through some old photos of me as a child. I noticed photos of me cheekily smiling, dancing around my house, swimming at the beach. That kid had a real carefree nature about him. He would swagger around in his speedo or a lion costume without a care, even with a proud scar on his tummy. Maybe it was time to channel little Tom's energy and be a bit kinder to myself. As a little kid, it is very easy to strut around with confidence and not give a care what others think.

Who's to say the adult me couldn't do the same?

After watching some episodes of cartoon television, I became inspired. I rushed and got out a piece of paper, along with my finest ballpoint pen. Standing in front of the mirror, I then wrote down each thing I didn't like about myself in the wackiest way possible. Here were some of my best observations, brace yourselves:

'The great equator lies on your stomach.'

'Your toes are like stubby little champagne corks.'

'You have a face for radio.'

Okay, that last one wasn't true, but it's one of my favourite punchlines to ever exist. This utterly bizarre description of myself led to a very wild caricature appearing on the other side of that mirror. I then burst out laughing at this exercise and began to realise that what we see in the mirror does not always show what we truly are.

In my personal experiences, I have grown great appreciation for body positivity and how every one of us has unique features and characteristics.

Slowly but surely, I began feeling more comfortable in my appearance and made it a mission to trust myself. Negative thoughts and cognitive distortions still appeared. The dilemma was no longer about whether I loved myself or not, it was whether I listened to my inner voice or ignored its pointed advice.

During my bouts of initial anxiety at university, I realised that I began to have utterly unrealistic expectations about my body. I wanted to magnetic, to be the man people looked at and thought looked like a million bucks. The reality is, I was determined to be the leading role in a perfect Hollywood fantasy. My reality was, I was a university student not happy with himself to the point it drove him crazy.

At one of our lectures about the wonders of child developmental theory, I noticed a stark internal shift. As my lecturer showed photos and videos of infants and children learning to socially interact, I thought back to little Tom. I thought back to the kid who would strut around in the middle aisles of a Hi-5 concert and shout every single word without caring what other parents might think. I needed to be that kid again.

I needed to take back my body, for me.

My parents were my biggest support in this endeavour, both being active people themselves. Conversations with my father planted vital steps to my current routine. I was determined to get started with exercise and fitness. Not for vanity, but for an internal sense of calm and peace. Dad repeatedly suggested I should go for a run and get some fresh air.

Like every seventeen-year-old boy, I thought I knew better. I did not want to partake in running due to similar self-doubt about how people would observe me while driving by in their cars. I often liked going on walks though, so maybe this was a natural starting point.

Soon enough, walks around Light Street Reserve became commonplace. I would try to make the time for at least 3-4 walks a week, ranging somewhere from half an hour to ninety minutes. I would often listen to music to try and distract from whatever chaos was happening in my world that day. Initially, it was scary. But with repeated practice and progress, being in that space became regular to me. I enjoyed going for walks and being in my own little world while enjoying the natural one around me. Walking was a good start, but maybe there was some other form of exercise I could do to help reach my goals.

After much nagging and persistence from my parents, I joined the ECU gym. Admittedly, I had never set foot in a gym except a few times in high school. But I knew that if I wanted to see change in my body image, I needed to take that risk.

Initially, I made it my life's work to sneak in there un-noticed by my peers. The biggest breakthrough didn't come through exercise though; it came through being honest with myself. I remember going through my induction with a trainer and feeling quite optimistic about my new routine. I knew that going to the gym would be tough and a commitment, but I also knew that this was about working through the negativity I felt surrounding my body.

So, for a few months, I regularly went to the gym and immediately followed my plan of weights, cardio and some light stretching. It felt good challenging myself and trying something different. My internal mindset went from questioning the size of my legs or the absence of abs to telling myself that I was making great baby steps.

I gained a bit of confidence back after those initial gym sessions, I soon realised that the problem wasn't that I had an ugly body, but that I only chose to see it in that way. Due to my newfound bravado and happiness in my routine, I decided to start taking photos of my body to help map the progress I was making. I looked back on those photos in the same way I looked at that photo album weeks ago, and I saw something. Big Tom had the same grin, the same silly exterior that Little Tom once did many years ago. I smiled from ear to ear in the realisation that progress was the necessary direction, not perfection. I knew that a perfect body does not exist, but that my perfect body was the one I had held on to this entire time.

Going to the gym and my workout journey naturally had its days of mistrust and dishonesty, I would sometimes workout for 20 minutes instead of an hour or find reasons to not be happy with my progress. In the long term, making an effort to exercise and to keep myself grounded led me to feel more comfortable in my own skin.

I had begun to take the mirror back. I took back my body. Progress for me was key, but so was honesty. I wanted to exercise and treat my body in a way that was suited for me. For me, my outlet was working out. I would regularly take photos of my chest and torso to track progress, and journal about my feelings working out, as well as my overall outlook on my body. The issue for me with my body wasn't about not looking strong enough, it was about not looking organised. In my mind, my sometimes-scruffy fashion choices and middling hygiene made me look ugly. But I overcame that roadblock through making myself uncomfortable and sitting with my discomfort.

There was no magic switch I could flip or spell I could cast to make me love myself again. Keeping promises to myself and being true to the progress I was making allowed the process to feel natural and rewarded. My self-respect and satisfaction I felt with my body felt earned, not simply handed to me.

Soon, people began to compliment me.

'You look like you've been working out.'

'I love the way your hair looks.'

'You've got such a lean figure.'

As a young man who was struggling to be sure in himself, it felt nice receiving this feedback from others. The real feedback I sought though had not yet arrived. Maybe, it never would. As time went on, I had days and weeks where I would skip the gym out of tiredness or sheer lack of motivation. But I had to keep reminding myself that I was not quitting on myself, but merely waiting for the right moment to try again.

I hated how discomfort felt, but I knew I couldn't keep running from it. I didn't like the situation I was in, but knew there was little point avoiding it for much longer.

My relationship with my body didn't transform overnight. It wasn't a quick fix. It grew slowly, muddled and sometimes backwards. Self-image is not a destination you arrive at and stay with, it is a moving target, a growing journey. The stories we tell ourselves when no one is listening can do more impact than we realise. Some days the mirror we look into will be kind. Other times it will be cruel and unforgiving. Neither version is really telling the truth.

The mirror doesn't report facts; it narrates what it wants to see. For a long time, I believed it.

Learning to live with the discomfort around my body, rather than trying to eradicate it, was the real change. I didn't chase perfection or wait to be ready. I just tried to show up for myself anyways. My body was treated with respect, even on days I really didn't like myself. Especially on those days.

My mirror still talks.

I just don't let it decide the story anymore.

ONE OF ONE, IRREPLACEABLE

If you could change yourself tomorrow, what would make
you better?
For the longest time, I had an answer prepared.
I would often catch myself comparing - my life, my interests,
my voice, to someone else's.
Every time I did, I would completely miss one vital point:
There is no one else like me.
Even if there was, they haven't lived my life.
No one else talks like me.
No one else sees the world how I do.
For a while, I saw this as a problem.
Being me meant being different.
I felt I had to tone myself down, to adjust myself until it
became acceptable.
The moment I stopped trying to fix myself, something shifted.
I realised I wasn't behind.
I was just different.
Being different wasn't something to correct, but something to
understand.
I know now that I was never missing anything but instead
looking for validation in the wrong things.
I wanted to be chosen.
To be approved.
To feel like I fit in.
I was too close to the story I kept telling myself.
I don't need to sound like anyone else.
I don't need to please anyone else.
I need to be who I already am.
Who I had been this whole time.

CHAPTER EIGHT
UNPLUGGED

My nightly routine used to look a lot different.

I would be bathed in a sea of blue light, scrolling endlessly on Instagram, desperate to get a slice of what pandemonium was going on in the world. Usually, the sounds of YouTube videos would provide sufficient background noise to my scrolling habits. It started out as ten or twenty minutes before bed, a way to catch a glimpse of global events or excitement.

Now, it has evolved to no shorter than an hour.

I used to find reasons to nitpick, to compare myself to the things I saw on my screen. I would see other people travelling to beloved sights across our globe, people celebrating the small joys in their lives. It got me thinking.

Why are people so invested in broadcasting their story this way? What do they get out of it?

The chase. The feeling of being part of the wider world. The fear of missing out on updates and exclusivity you could find almost anywhere else.

You will never believe how fast time can fly when your eyes are glued to a screen. My endless cycle of scrolling late into the night and repeating the trick when I wake is something I have been slowly trying to phase out of my life. It isn't always as easy as it looks.

How could it not be so addicting? We scroll and scroll, hoping to get a glimpse into the wonderful things others are doing, and to be right on top of any global news or trends.

I often struggled with balancing my social media use in high school. Due to my competitive and sometimes jealous nature, I would tend to use Instagram as a benchmark for what I see in the real world. Every time I saw a post from someone my age, my sense of self-worth would take a hit. To me, seeing even fifty, one hundred people liking their post meant that they were miles ahead of where I'd ever be. I would feel an unhealthy mix of jealousy and frustration.

To me, lavishness meant success. If someone my age posted a photo on vacation or at a fancy place locally, my brain would automatically assume that they had their life together. What you see on social media platforms including Instagram or TikTok is what people choose to upload and make public. But as a teenager, I refused to accept that vital truth.

Becoming a part of the social landscape seemed scary to me. Soon however, the world in the palm of my hand made me desperate to remain in touch with the day-to-day change of popular culture. On days I wouldn't otherwise be preoccupied by work or school, I consistently spent solid half-hour blocks scrolling through Instagram. Occasionally, I would set downtime limits for my phone, but that still was not enough to block me from the excitement of seeing the droves of new information online.

My battles with social media usually followed a similar pattern. Check my notifications obsessively whenever I posted or messaged someone, compare with others when they posted, and take the numbers I saw in response to my posts as true validation. Due to my overwhelm and constant stressors about how I was perceived online and in real life, I found it very easy to treat what I saw online as gospel and the unabashed truth.

It became a difficult choice what side I would show of myself on social media. I eventually decided to blend my thoughts on social media to use it intentionally. I made a personal commitment to myself in Year 11 to use Instagram for good and post the parts of my life I wanted to be seen. This change in mindset worked, I had let go of my cynical nature around social media and was actively working towards seeing the use of it more positively.

But I soon cracked.

When people make content for a desired audience, it is very easy to pick apart their latest post or message and relate it somehow to our own lives.

Excessive social media use and online validation can cause multiple negative impacts on our wellbeing. My own battles with social media usage and comparison saw me feel intense bouts of anger, jealousy and resentment towards others.

Friends. Family. People I barely knew.

Due to seeing what great things others were supposedly doing in their lives, I took their online personas as reality, and in turn, started to become more distrusting of others. I became very irritated and unhappy with the level of social experiences they were supposedly having. If I saw someone wearing a nice t-shirt or a trendy piece of clothing, I would internally elevate their status above my own. My refusal to differentiate the digital world from real life achievements saw me become egotistical and quite unnerving of others.

Ignoring these feelings of invalidation became a severe problem. Since social media is very easily accessible, it requires very little effort to access all corners of the world with a few keystrokes. I wanted to have the same prestige or social charisma I thought others had purely due to the content and messages they would spread online as glimpses of their life.

However, I chose to ignore these feelings. I let them fester and I didn't bother to look inwards to understand more about how I felt towards my relationship with social media. This led to me wiping my Instagram profile and deleting the app from my phone for the entirety of Year 12.

Deleting social media from my devices cost me access to the world, but it brought me peace. I didn't delete social media because I hated it, but because I hated who I became when I used it.

It was during this year of digital detox that I learned a vital realisation about social media and its ability to warp our view of the world.

Everyone is living on their own timeline.

It is incredibly easy for social media to be seen as the place where we can feel the most validated. The growing rise in likes, followers and comments can provide us with an external sense of adrenaline we never thought possible. Yet we as the people on the ground use these metrics as ways to measure our self-worth.

What you see online is someone else's timeline, it is a glimpse of where they are currently at in their life. They may choose to present it with vacation photos, or prophetic paragraphs about optimism for the future. When you see an engagement post, or a post about that new startup business, do not use it as a metric for your own success. Be it in our career, relationships, our hobbies, we are all unique - how we reach our level of success looks vastly different from person to person.

I have talked a lot in this chapter about the downsides of social media and have perhaps been slightly biased due to my own experiences. However, it is important to remember that our growth happens offline.

Social media can also be used creatively to find purpose or inspiration. One of my favourite examples of this is through Pinterest. I often search Pinterest to find photos that beautifully capture the natural world. Sometimes for screensavers, some for playlist covers, others for enjoyment and genuine curiousity. Pinterest is an incredible community for people to share their own creative ideas and find their creative niche. Inspiration on social media can also be found through its admirable nature to allow people in sharing their stories. Platforms such as TikTok and Snapchat provide ways for people to connect with relatives or friends across the entire globe.

The main way to use social media more positively is to not let it run your life. I have all social media apps deleted from my phone. I only access them using the Safari web browser app on my phone. This reduces the urge I once had to visit Instagram and Facebook constantly throughout my day, allowing it to be lost in a sea of other websites and links. This in turn helped limit the amount of time I spent doomscrolling, spending hours online searching through things other people had posted. I often use short timers for 10 or 15 minutes to dedicate that time purely to scrolling social media apps. Then, I try my best to pivot.

When we measure our progress against the highlights of others, we forget to appreciate the small wins happening right in front of us.

Nothing changed online for me. The posts still existed. I just stopped letting them decide how I felt about my own life.

If we can be patient with our progress in real time, we should be just as patient with ourselves online.

CHAPTER NINE
IT'S ALL IN YOUR HEAD

'I feel like I hide behind my thoughts.'

My therapist Christian hunched over in his chair, his face turning from an expression of intent to an expression of intrigue.

'You say you hide behind your thoughts. What does that mean?'

My hands clenched tighter, my legs started to shake, my eyes tightened as I took a deep breath. My mind instantly races, considering how to properly articulate the wave of negative judgements I let myself listen to daily.

'Well…at times I feel quite anxious about the simplest things. How I walk into a room, if people are judging me for what I wear, my facial features…'

'Why do you feel this way?'

'I guess I want to be seen as perfect.'

'And why does that matter to you so much?'

'Because I need everyone to know how hard I work.'

That sentence was the very state of mind I carried in early 2022, I was halfway through my university degree, recently coping with an ugly fallout from a crush gone astray. The sense of judgement and stress I felt towards myself seemed more real than it had ever been.

Whether it be based on our self-image or external factors, our brains will always find many, if albeit blurry, reasons to overthink everything. My personal journey with anxiety has taught me that your anxiety does not control you, that you are not the thoughts inside your head.

For me, a large deal of these anxious behaviours were ways to mask my shame surrounding my lack of confidence in myself. As human beings, we can consistently feel pressure about how we are viewed by others. We are growing up in a world that can be overstimulating due to our heavy culture of comparison and pressure to have life figured out early. It is only through discomfort that we learn the most about ourselves and how to best process our negative thoughts and attitudes of self.

The act of actively using your anxiety to build your self-confidence is one of time, process and discipline. My journey of owning my battle with anxiety first came through learning to open up through therapy. I used to really struggle with articulating my thoughts and letting people know exactly how I felt within myself.

The problem with trying to escape my anxiety was that I was concerned no one would understand what I was going through. Mum and Dad were always happy to try and support me wherever they could, they would give valuable advice on how to gain confidence by trying new things, and the importance of staying true to myself.

Midway through my second year of university, I decided that it would be best to talk to someone external, someone on the outside who could give me valuable advice and tools from their experience. Therapy wasn't new to me; I had gone to a counsellor in high school during my late teen years. It was through these initial conversations in high school that I learned to open up and to trust my feelings as being valid.

For about three to four months, I visited a clinic not too far from my house. I remember the anxious wait while filling in client paperwork, worried to see what person would be dissecting my mental psyche. Soon, I met my therapist, Christian. He was in his forties with two children and had experience of several decades. It was clear from the off that Christian was an honest character. He could often tell if I was using my anxiety to get out of things cheaply or wasn't thinking about things in the best possible way.

Although it took me a while to get fully comfortable, I appreciated the time and attention Christian gave me when it came to discussing such first world problems including my dating worries, sibling rivalry and struggles with my appearance. It was refreshing to hear from a different perspective who could encourage me to look at things differently.

All my life I have found dealing with my anxiety particularly difficult. I never could identify quite where it came from. My anxiety would always show up in the loudest of ways, just as it shows up differently for many people. Quite often it would present itself in negative thoughts, ways that I would convince myself that whatever step I would need to take could somehow break me.

'You're not good enough.'

'What if they laugh because you walk on your toes?'

'Why is your nose so big?'

I often felt a deep fear of being judged or being too much for people. Due to the results of my surgery at birth, I became quite self-conscious of my appearance and my mannerisms. As a child I would often walk on my toes due to having tight calf muscles, and this led to me needing casts on my legs to help me walk properly. This became a point of stress for me early on.

I was quite a shy boy growing up and especially in primary school. Whenever confronted with the idea of change or meeting new people, I would go deep into my shell. I was often reluctant to make new friends growing up. Not because I didn't want to meet new people, but just because I was scared of being judged, as most young people are.

Year 7 English was the first real chance my anxiety had to make itself overtly known to my peers. Our first assessment was to write a short story and read it orally to the class. I had written a story about a grandfather who tells him a brief recap of their family history, to show how generations are connected through tradition. I was proud of my effort and felt confident when rehearsing it in front of my parents. The writing part I felt happy about, because I knew I could articulate my ideas well with a structure and careful planning.

The public speaking part was the aspect of this task that daunted me overwhelmingly. When it came my time to present, I instantly got shivers. My teacher reassured me that everything would be okay and that everyone gets a bit nervous sometimes. She gave me a calming nod as the eyes of the other boys locked squarely with mine.

It was time to tell my story.

'Once upon a time.....'

'Once....upon...'

'Once.....'

My eyes welled up as the worry became too much. I sprinted

out of the room a nervous wreck.

I was afraid of being judged during public speaking. When I was with other partners presenting to a group, I felt comfortable, I could almost hide behind them. But when I was up there on my own, that's when the waves of panic would hit. I was scared that people would laugh at me, that I would stumble my lines, or that I would lose track of my thoughts. Now through daily practice as a teacher, I have definitely come around to the idea of public speaking.

I also would be quite hesitant to put my hand up in class, of a great fear that I would say the wrong answer or risk offending someone. Whenever my parents would order food and I would usually be with them, I often became quite timid and scared to order things, hiding behind my parents for comfort.

As I matured, I had come to grips with the fact that my anxiety was a problem, and I needed help. Naturally, I am quite a stubborn person, reluctant to ask for help or support, even if it is profusely clear I need some guidance.

I very much like to do things my own way.

Due to my anxiety about various self-imposed negative biases, I began quite hesitant to ask for help about my mental struggles. You could say I had anxiety about my anxiety.

How's that for some irony?

My anxiety wasn't largely just due to how I interacted with others or how I presented myself, it was largely through a need for validation, for safety and for assurance that I was doing well. This resistance to do something about my endless worries led me down a dark spiral as I progressed through high school. I started to think more paranoid thoughts, in a state of being on edge about what others thought of me.

Therapy was a place that soon became safe to me. Through school and even at university, I found that consistent practice and a willingness to be uncomfortable allowed me to open up and be honest about my thoughts. The cost of my anxiety had become far too great to handle. Lost confidence and a negative state of mind led me to finally seek courage.

Every conversation pointed to the same thing – my standards were too high. My counsellors in high school made it very clear, in no uncertain terms, that I needed to let go of the unrealistic metrics I held myself too.

But as to how I went about doing that, this was a bit of a

puzzle. It became clear through my initial sessions with Christian that I spoke quite harshly to myself. In my first session with Christian, he made me say out loud the negative things I had been telling myself. This is where it got very real, very quickly.

'You'll never amount to anything unless you're the best.'

'You're different to the others.'

'No one will take you seriously.'

Ouch.

As I rattled off each negative and self-destructive thought, my mind began to ease. I felt a weight lift off my shoulders as I verbalised my thoughts out loud, rather than simply keeping them in. I hadn't said those thoughts loud to anyone, but in my head, they became all I could hear. Christian then asked me something very interesting.

'Would you ever say these words to someone else?'

'No, of course not.' I replied.

Isn't it crazy how the thoughts we keep inside about ourselves, the ones we would never say out loud, can make us hurt the most?

Yet we would never ever dare say these to anyone else, because let's face it, we'd do serious damage.

That's when it hit me.

I was so unkind and cruel to myself through my words, and my words had seriously raw power. It was through more sessions with Christian that I began to see clearer the reason for this negative self-talk. The reason I spoke so negatively to myself is because I was only choosing to focus on the negatives in my life, I overgeneralised how bad things were.

I came to see that my negative self-talk was the root of my anxiety. My intense worries about my life and future came from the narrative I was telling myself. Christian gave me two strong strategies to help me with my anxiety about myself. I would love to share these with you now. These strategies are simple and have helped me calm my worries about various things over the years.

The first strategy Christian gave me was to question myself. For example, I expressed a negative thought I had about failing my second-year work experience (or 'prac' as it's known in education). He then instructed me to ask one question of myself. 'How likely is that?' I stopped to consider my thinking. The reality is I had been working hard to create engaging lessons for my prac and was making an effort to ensure that I was presenting myself appropriately, so I had no reason to fear. He then asked me another question 'So what?'

I had never thought of that. He was right.

For example, if I failed or got a low result, there was always the option to repeat it or ask for feedback. Reminding myself that there were always multiple options to any scenario, that anything can happen, was the internal shift I needed. I for so long had been thinking of things in black and white, that things could only go one way. I had to consider all perspectives when my worries overcame me. I then got into the habit of asking myself these two questions whenever I had an overwhelming negative thought.

By asking myself these questions and taking a more cavalier attitude to approaching my anxieties, it allowed me to truly consider whether there was really any reason to fear. I soon used this approach for all sorts of stressors, including worries about people judging me for my outfits, as well as worries about friendships. It really made things easier to have a mental process to go through that was quick and easy. This helped me to calm my mind and realise that sometimes I would overreact about my concerns.

The second strategy Christian gave me was to write down all of my anxious thoughts at the end of the day, or when I had some spare time to think. After I wrote down all my negative thoughts and concerns, Christian instructed me to circle all the thoughts that I could control or had any power over. Through this exercise, I discovered something startling. I only circled one or two of about fifty negative thoughts. The reality is that we can only control so much, and we fret so much over the things out of our control. Some things will happen without our knowledge or action, and some things happen because we choose to let them.

Reframing my negative thoughts and being willing to let myself sit with discomfort helped me realise a vital truth. I realised through these exercises that my thoughts didn't define me, that I was stronger than my mental judgements.

My anxiety forced me to look inwards and eventually face my fears. I knew that I couldn't let my insecurities take me down, that I had to work on creating a safe space to let them become more acknowledged. I still get nervous and stressed about things day to day, everyone does. But now I am more confident in taking a step back and finding more reasons to be positive and kinder to myself.

Looking back now, I don't see my anxiety as something that held me back. I see it as something that finally forced me to encounter myself properly. My anxiety proved where I was hurt, where I was insecure, and where I was trying too hard to be someone I thought others wanted. As uncomfortable as those moments were, they made me more self-aware and more honest about who I am.

I still have anxious days. I still overthink things I probably shouldn't. But the difference now is that I don't let those thoughts scare me the way they used to. I acknowledge them. I sit with them. I let them float on by. Anxiety taught me that peace isn't the absence of internal noise, rather learning not to believe all you hear.

My anxiety never disappeared.

I just refused to let it dictate my actions anymore.

CHAPTER TEN
EMBRACING THE STORM

I slammed my laptop shut and threw my bag across my bedroom.

My fists were heavily clenched, breath heavy and short.

As I began to consider what would await me, my eyes narrowed as they met with the mirror. Tears began to stream down my face as I questioned exactly what I was doing in my dream career. My mind raced with realisation and doubt.

'Just get through today.'

'What's done is done, you can't change the past.'

'You're supposed to know what you're doing by now.'

This is how days would usually start for me at work. I am a primary school teacher, one of many tasked with guiding the next generation of future leaders. My first formal teaching position was teaching Year Three at a private school in the Perth hills. As a product of Catholic education myself, I was chomping at the bit to get started in what seemed like a very fitting first placement. I would soon come to realise the reality of my dream career was more testing than tantalising.

It started off well enough, with my freshly minted optimism proving to be a real drawcard with my class of twenty-eight bubbly thinkers. I was told by some my class was one of the toughest in the school. My naivety and arrogance suggested that I would be able to rectify specific behavioural issues with a gentle nature and clear expectations. Granted, my Year 3's were a lovely bunch of children and made me fortunate for my position.

From the jump my focus was being able to relate to these kids. I wanted to make them feel like they could be themselves, and that there was room to make mistakes and try again. Emotional and social regulation was my initial focus for my class, particularly for those children who needed extra support.

On my very first day, I instantly became flooded with questions about myself. Kids can be very inquisitive people. 'I'm trying to read your name badge; can we call you Thomas?' Their eyes clearly saw my name badge printed in fine black font. I felt like I was being interrogated. The truth is though; I didn't mind all the questions and comments. I was happy to answer most questions my kids asked me about myself, as it made me appear more human. I thought that my kids deserved to know a bit about me.

My students were incredibly creative and great critical thinkers. I also loved how there was a clear sense of camaraderie amongst my students. They were happy to speak their mind and ask questions without a fear of being judged by their peers.

Being a 22-year-old graduate responsible for 28 little intellects was always going to be an exciting challenge. From the offset it became very clear which groups or cliques there were in our classroom. The boys chose to be sat in the back corner of the room in their crew, with the girls sparsely spread across the room next to their friends. Despite the fact there were more girls in that room, you better believe the boys weren't afraid to make themselves known.

This sense of friendship also extended to our regular morning meetings as a class. Every day, the students would walk into the classroom excitedly and chat to their friends, sometimes not paying attention to the clear instruction of sitting on the mat. Their constant fervour and energy sometimes made it hard to start the day, but sometimes it was nice to see them interact and be happy about socialising with others.

I knew immediately that I would need to do some serious research and put time into figuring how to get on top of my class. Routinely, some students took it upon themselves to call out over me, say derogatory things to their classmates, and use the room as their own private jungle gym. I managed this as best I could, following protocol with verbal warnings and loss of privileges. Nothing worked.

Afternoons were spent kicking and screaming, mornings were spent pacing up and down while my legs buckled under the pressure. Pressure not placed on by anyone else, but by myself. In my mind I had to make sure this first year ran perfectly, or else it would be a colossal embarrassment if I failed at my first hurdle.

Monday afternoons were particularly tricky, two hours of hyperactive eight and nine-year-olds at peak energy was a trickier roadblock than first thought. Time would often be wasted waiting for kids to line up properly, despite repeated reminders from myself and leadership staff of how such routines should be performed. At staff meetings, I regularly recall slouching in my chair and feeling utterly depleted at the thought of even turning up to school the next day.

Most nights I spent tossing and turning, the recounts of incidents and altercations scattering around my mind, telling me I was in over my head.

'Stay calm.' I would tell myself.

'You can do this. You are human.'

'No one gets it right the first time.'

For a job that is considered fulfilling, I never truly could switch off.

One Thursday afternoon late in Term 3, I foolishly decided that I was ready to leave it all on the field. I was determined to stamp on constant behavioural problems and defiance, even if it meant showing a side of me not one person has seen.

After one lunchtime, a group of the boys in my class were arguing about an incident at a soccer game a few minutes prior. One of the boys allegedly called the other a cheater, and insults were being hurled across the classroom. This student had slowly been chipping away at my teddy bear exterior for months with his unique approach to classroom communication. Sensing some unease, I instantly took the culprit outside where we began to have a civil chat about name-calling and how our words have power. Our words most definitely hold some power, but for how long?

As I spoke to the boy while the rest of my class was partaking in some silent reading, chatter emerged in earshot.

'Shhhh….shhhh… be quiet when Mr. Robertson walks in.'

'Mr. Robertson's not going to do anything about it, he's too soft.'

'Why can't we just have a normal classroom?'

That last one stung. A lot.

As I attempted to hear this boy's story of why he used such

hurtful language to a peer, my body went limp. My face was feverish as sweat poured down my cheeks and forehead. It wasn't long before my blood boiled. My fists shook, my curious and wry smile twisted into a snarl. My calves tightened as I breathed heavier than I thought possible. Tears began to form, my entire body pulsed. This was uncharted territory.

I turned my head and swung the door open. Twenty-seven pairs of little eyes immediately locked with mine. This was the point of no return.

I stomped through the doorway, narrowed my eyes and let out an almighty roar.

'That is enough, SIT DOWN! I am trying to have a conversation with another student. How rude and disrespectful.'

Silence fell over my entire class. I had never seen them so shocked. I had never yelled before, to anyone. Until that moment.

You could hear a pin drop.

Widened eyes and opened mouths met my eyes as those little bodies couldn't believe what they were seeing.

Some children stared back aghast, others avoided eye contact.

Embarrassment rattled through my bones. Weeks of trying and testing new ideas had all gone to waste. It seemed like I was a lost cause.

Soon, I turned back outside to continue my conversation with this anger-stricken little boy. Laughter began to emerge from the classroom. I had never felt so defeated. I paused mid conversation, sent the child back inside, and slumped in an almighty collapse. I immediately felt regret. I didn't want to yell. But I didn't want to work that day either.

Days, weeks, months of bubbling unresolved emotional angst had come unstuck in that one moment. As I dropped my children off at the school's gym for their sport lesson, I took a deep breath, looked around the school grounds, and let out an almighty sigh.

'I've just blown my chance at getting them onside.'

'They'll never trust me.'

'I've just made a fool of myself.'

As I drove home that afternoon, I thought back to the day's events. Those coarsely screamed words replaying over in my mind, as a reminder of the damaging I had probably caused to the children who found enjoyment in attending such a lovely school. I made no phone calls, no music played. The silence spoke much louder that afternoon. It was on this very car ride home that I came across a startling truth.

My emotions were so aggressive because I had not properly listened to them. When my inner voice was crying out for help to be cared for, I chose to ignore it and power through. I knew deep down that I should listen to my emotions and take my reactions as clues for how I was pushing down negativity and resentment. Yet, I chose to ignore, because to me being a good teacher meant having it altogether. It was when I wanted things to be together, that they crumbled in an enormous heap.

I didn't understand why I felt that way, I just knew that I needed to make a change. One of the most important things I have learned in my studies as an educator is that our emotions are reactions to events, not a true depiction of our whole life circumstance. This is the same for school children as it is for adults. Our emotions are the product of a moment, not the sum of our own faults.

The more we ignore our emotions, the more destructive they can become when they finally make themselves known. By keeping our emotions in, we are actively forgoing the chance to be honest with ourselves. Being honest with what our emotions represent allows for greater satisfaction in processing daily events or situations that affected us.

The hardest part about being a teacher for me was finding the time to truly process each day. The nature of that first year was so touch and go it became a mix of deadlines, regrets and bad decisions due to my inexperience.

I spent that Thursday afternoon decompressing once I returned home. I ate some chocolate to put my body at ease, and took the time to watch YouTube in a warm bath, just as I did on tough days like this one. I then continued my usual afternoon routine by briefly looking over my notes for the next day's lesson and meticulously preparing mentally for how I would conclude yet another week. Not long after, I went to sleep and began to again relay negative self-talk in my mind, not letting myself off easy for a stressful day.

This was pretty typical for my afternoon routine, decompress and distract. I chose to focus on the next day's grind rather than focus on the current day's hurt. But, I couldn't put it off any longer.

That Friday morning, I began to do some serious reflection on my way to school. I decided that positivity was going to be the soundtrack of my day as I became mentally battle ready. However, I knew that I could not move on and have a great Friday without first unpacking a disastrous Thursday before. I had to stop running away from my mistakes and check in with how I was feeling. I began to talk to myself.

'Yesterday was tough, I felt angry.'

'I felt angry when things went wrong, I overreacted.'

'Today when things go wrong, I can take deep breaths.'

'I can scan the room, I can think of something funny to distract from the negativity.'

'Today I am going to show up for myself and think positively. Nothing is going to let me get in my head.'

That morning, the energy was different. My kids came to school with beaming smiles on their faces and I felt a shift in myself too. Yesterday was not the best day, but I was determined to change things. In our usual morning meeting, my children sat down in front of me as I gathered my thoughts. I wasted zero time.

'How would we say yesterday went, Year 3's?'

The hands shot up.

Responses such as bad, not good and disappointing came to mind from my students.

'So, we know yesterday was not a great day. Mr. Robertson had a difficult day yesterday and perhaps didn't show his frustration in the best way. I'm sorry for getting so upset. That wasn't right.'

My kids immediately gave reassuring smiles back at me, as if to say that they knew where I was coming from.

'Sometimes, even as adults, it can be really hard to manage our feelings. Even the really big ones that can sometimes seem scary or confronting.'

'We are nearly at the end of Term 3, I know everyone is feeling tired, I am certainly feeling it too. But I want you all to know I am very proud for all your effort you keep showing. Of course we'll have difficult days, but we can always try again the next time.'

I had deliberated on my own emotions for too long, but I hadn't yet considered the feelings of my students.

'I want to hear from you though guys, how are we feeling about things right now?'

Some students began to share their stresses of balancing commitments with their homework and school. Others shared their optimism about the holidays but overall tiredness after nine weeks of nonstop work. These were all very relatable feelings.

'Thank you all for sharing. I needed to hear that.'

'It seems we're all feeling a bit tired. I know when Mr. Robertson gets tired, I usually get a bit cranky.'

The children all nodded, both in agreement and acknowledgement of their own reactions to tiredness.

'When Mr. Robertson was driving home yesterday, he began to have a think to himself about some useful things I could do when I am tired.'

'I like to ask myself two very important questions.'

'Number One: How am I feeling?'

'Number Two: Why do I feel this way?'

After this chat, I sensed the mood lift in my room. The biggest breakthrough came later in the day. I noticed during our Maths lesson that morning one of the girls in my room became agitated with her table partner, she was slamming books and folding her arms in a huff.

'Let's have a chat outside, shall we?'

She nodded as tears began to stream down her face.

This girl began to divulge information about friendship issues that had been occurring, she claimed two other female students were giving her a hard time and she felt helpless in the situation.

'Okay, I hear you, and I understand, that would be very frustrating.'

She continued.

'I feel upset and angry.' She answered Question 1 with no prompting; that's an attentive student.

'That's completely understandable, can you tell me why?'

'The other girls call me names and there's always issues between us, on both sides really.'

I racked my brain to figure out what the solution to this long-standing problem could be. I was determined to solve it on my own accord.

'Sometimes friends can fight, and that's okay! It isn't easy to always agree with your friends, but friends will always have your back. You have explained to me that you feel sad or angry. I am so proud of you for explaining how you feel, that isn't easy.' She smiled after this little dose of encouragement.

'You can't change what has happened, all you can do is tell yourself that although you feel down, this doesn't mean that everything is suddenly terrible. You just have to say, yes I feel sad, but I know this will pass.'

She offered her sincere thanks before darting back into the classroom.

Then, it clicked in my head.

'If I am giving my students advice on how to process their emotions, especially at such a young age, why can't I live by my words?'

I had figured through observing my students that our emotions while volatile can be extremely useful. They are immediate reactions and displays of things we haven't yet processed. Often, we feel a need to burst right away rather than taking the time to understand exactly what is going on in our head. That is the lesson my students taught me that day, true courage comes from embracing the chaos, not just watching it happen with no answer.

That afternoon, my students convened on the oval for Class Sport, often a chance for the kids to run around and blow off steam, a chance for us teachers to catch some much-needed fresh air.

At this time, my kids complained that the other Year 3/4 class were playing their own game of dodgeball and that we were not included or notified about their activities. The reason for this being our class took a little longer to come from the classroom than usual. Normally, I would possibly send a student over to the other class to ask if we could play. But all I could muster was a sincere apology. 'I'm really sorry, I didn't know about it either.'

My whistle blew, the voices ceased.

'I completely understand everyone is frustrated about the dodgeball situation. I know how much we love a good game of dodgeball on a Friday afternoon, especially with other classes.'

'We feel upset and angry because we weren't included, which is no one's fault.'

'There's nothing we can do to change the past, right?'

'All we can do is accept we feel frustrated but try to make the best of our Friday afternoon.'

'I know everyone's a little annoyed, but that's no way to spend a Friday afternoon. We've acknowledged we feel a bit flat, why don't we let our emotions out? Free play for everyone!'

My children erupted with an almighty roar. They were excited. I was proud of how I handled that exchange. The angry, unchecked Mr. Robertson would have let my emotions show and tried to bite back at my kids. But I took my own advice and unpacked our shared emotions as a group, and from the looks on my students' faces, they appreciated this little exercise.

That first year of teaching was far from perfect and yes, at times difficult. It taught me a lot about resilience and how to find happiness when things don't go your way. I learned valuable lessons about acknowledging your emotions, sitting with them and engaging in self-talk about why these emotions are present. Understanding my own emotions in such a way helped me relate to my students better. By understanding my own thoughts more, I was able to more comfortably engage with my students and other staff, having more honest conversations.

Only when we sit with our feelings, those furious glances, and those moments of accepting fault, can we truly become more empathetic to ourselves. When I shrieked at my students, I reached a brutal realisation.

I hadn't been listening to myself at all.

It took years of practice, mental unpacking and honest critiquing of myself to fully understand my emotions. I still have days and weeks where things get tough. Losing control of emotions although daunting, is a natural occurrence. Our emotional bandwidth can only tend to so much in our lives. I still haven't solved my emotional woes or days of doubt, and maybe we aren't supposed to.

My truth is that I am emotional. I am dramatic. But I am not apologetic. Embracing my thoughts, even the troubling ones, allowed me to further articulate just how I reacted to events. I did not change the way I reacted emotionally, nor did I suddenly have it all figured out.

That next week I stepped through the school gates, I noticed that discomfort. For the first time, I felt I was truly in control. No more just getting through the day, it was time to start embracing it.

BEAUTY OF FALLING

October 2025, I sat in the staff room after a heavy day.
It was time to find out. Had I done enough to stay next year?
I held my breath as I walked through the door, puffing my
chest like I belonged there.
My boss thanked me for my work. I could feel the moment
coming.
Then it did.
'We don't have a place for you next year. We feel more
experience is necessary.'
My shoulders dropped.
Someone else would be wearing these boots next year.
'Do you have any questions for us?'
No. Not out loud.
I kept smiling - the way you do when you don't want anyone
to feel awkward for hurting you.
The walk back to my classroom felt longer than it ever had.
Every step echoed.
I kept wondering which moment they decided I wasn't
enough.
It hurt more because deep down, I saw it coming.
Maybe this wasn't the end, just exposure.
I still had more to learn.
Being told I wasn't needed hurt. But it didn't mean I never
would be.
It exposed who I was when there was no applause.
This rejection allowed my ego to die a quiet death.
I walked out of that room without a job.
But also, without the illusion that I needed one to prove
something.
For the longest time, I needed to feel chosen.
That day, I realised I didn't.

CHAPTER ELEVEN
MATTERS OF THE HEART

I never knew what love truly meant.

So, I searched for its meaning in music.

Most days after university classes, I would spend my time in the computer lab, often finishing assessments, sometimes socialising. Other times a healthy and frequent mix of both worlds. The one constant when studying was the blue headphones that would caress my ears.

Some days, I would get lost in the lush melodies and rhythms filling my ears, and it would become impossible to focus on anything else. Some would say it's procrastination. Looking back, it felt more like realisation. I quite often liked to listen to acoustic music in such a setting, music that would calm me and put me at ease.

Often a very common theme would present itself.

Love.

Safety.

A sense of fulfillment in another person.

It should come as no surprise that listening to copious amounts of John Mayer will do that to a boy. His music, along with a healthy mix of Coldplay, The 1975 and Harry Styles made me take a step back and think about what a future of love would look like for me.

Ballads of heartbreak, longing and yearning that I would listen to in order to ease myself would make me consider what to me was at the time the one unanswered question in my life.

Would romantic love ever make its way to me?

I am quite the sucker for a love song. Not for its overtly cliché lyrics of wanting to be with someone until their last days, but for the feelings of warmth, optimism and growth they provide. There is so much depth and genuine sincerity to a song dedicated to the possibility of a future with someone special. Those songs provided me with comfort, a feeling of hope, and an overwhelming sense of well-intentioned paranoia.

Every time I would hear Chris Martin sing about feeling joy for the world and for the woman of his dreams, I would get butterflies. It made me think that maybe, one day, that could be me too. And how could I not? Love was all around at university. This came through people from my course forming friendships, as well as constantly observing genuine acts of kindness and compassion between strangers and causes. Witnessing such an open display of care and respect between people made me wonder if such a path was possible.

Admittedly, my understanding of love was quite naive. I only ever considered love to be a romantic connection. After all, that was the way the movies and music I consumed portrayed it. Forming crushes on girls at university and even through schooling didn't really help my limited understanding of one of our world's most relatable constructs.

I have learned as I have matured that love can mean many things. It can mean simply saying hello to someone, a warm hug, making someone a bowl of soup on a cold day. Love is not simply saying those well-known three little words. It is showing respect to others through a genuine want to support those we care about.

Friendships also taught me a crucial meaning of love. Throughout my life, I have been fortunate to form many healthy female and male friendships. For many young men, there is often a stigma around forming friendships with the opposite sex, that it automatically means romance or sexual attraction. The same stigma exists for young women too.

Why is it so hard to separate friendship from attraction in the eyes of an outsider?

We are taught from a young age that love mostly means holding hands, showing physical affection and meeting at the end of the aisle. As kids we are naturally wired to believe this is the only form of love that can exist in our world, forgoing other more natural forms of love including friendships, family relationships and love of our natural environment.

Looking back on my childhood, I see now that these friendships were put in my path to teach me about love through means of common interest. Friendships are quite often formed on the basis of having similar likes and dislikes to other people. What we are interested in, our shared loves if you will, help us form a much greater love between a group of people who simply want to spend more time embarking on lived experiences together.

Love means showing up for others in good times and bad. Through experiences such as grief, loss or sickness, love shines through when we connect with others. It shines through when we work to provide time and space for the people in our lives to heal their wounds.

One of the most common types of love I witnessed growing up was in fact romantic love. I have seen this in many forms, both through consummation of love, and parting of ways. The major lesson I have learned about romantic love is that it comes when you least expect. Romantic love is not purely romantic because of the overt physical and emotional expectations conveyed to us from a young age. It is romantic because of the changes we see within ourselves. Romantic love is a strong commitment to another person that you know is equally committed to you.

At its core, that's what love is, commitment.

I take great pride in being able to work through my own theories and meaning of love. Through some tough lessons about heartbreak and ignorance, as well as joyful moments of peace, I have realised that love is not one size fits all. How we see love in its many forms depends on how we view the importance of our connections to ourselves, people and our wider world.

My meaning of love as a boy was quite skewed towards romantic happy endings with a marriage and children. As a man, my meaning of love is balanced towards themes of comfort, reassurance and respect. This meaning evolved over time through reflections about how I show up in social interaction, as well as reflections on my ability to express my feelings of love to others.

I never truly accepted my new view on love until I reached my second or third year of university, when my head began to listen to my heart. From deep within myself, I knew that before I could feel love, I first had to let it show. I couldn't go looking for it or find it in high or low places. I had to let it arrive in its own organic way.

I am not ashamed to admit a relationship was always the goal for me, especially in high school. I was set on the idea of meeting a genuine lady and being able to live an exciting life with her. I've always found the idea of meeting someone new and getting to pick their brain such a fascinating exercise. As the saying goes, first impressions are everything.

I wanted the thrill of the chase, the feelings my favourite songwriters always poeticised. I could imagine the murmurs of excitement when meeting someone for the first time, the rush you get when they look into your eyes.

A man could only dream, right?

It seemed so glamorous, oh so perfect.

As luck would have it, I wouldn't have to wait too long after graduating high school. Being from an all-boys school, my interactions with the feminine sex were admittedly slim. But I was not going to university without trusting myself to make more connections. Not to be romantic. Just to make new friends, and if something more came of that, how great of a bonus.

I have never been the most social person, anyone who knows me would tell you I like to keep to myself and stay relatively low-profile. I managed to make quite a few genuine female friends at university, all lovely women who shared the same passion for change I did.

I honestly never really thought much of it romantically, except for one instance. I did try my hand at starting a potential friendship with one of these women, only to be rejected without any notice. That was a lot of texting I would never get back. I was absolutely dejected. I had put myself out there for what felt like the first time in a long time, only to be kept on edge and never given the closure I craved.

For months I was in fits of rage over this. I was upset over being dropped, being ignored, being forgotten with zero reason provided. Through this experience I learned to not force positive outcomes and to use the evidence in front of you as signals.

But I was not determined to let this wasted time get me down.

As luck would have it, an incredible opportunity would soon fall into my lap. I had been quite close friends with a girl ever since our degree started. We talked a lot at university and shared a lot of the same interests (my sincere regards to Mr. Harry Styles). I never considered a romantic connection between us until midway through our second year.

Aviva and I would talk to each other in each tutorial and university lecture. We'd offer each other passing nods and glances in the hallway. The choruses of mocking comments from our friends never really subsided, they still don't.

'You two would make a really cute couple.'

These words appeared over text almost a year later.

Admittedly, we had been flirting hard with each other, whether we want to admit it or not. I couldn't help it, she was beautiful and utterly genuine.

'If you don't take this step, you'll be kicking yourself.' I wisely said.

That August, as we strolled into the library, I requested her presence on a walk. Why I decided to take us back the other direction had a much deeper meaning than she realised.

I then launched into an eloquent and somewhat pre-prepared monologue about our friendship so far and explained how much I valued her closeness. We strolled around campus, taking in adored buildings and the sites we had spent time forming our strong connection.

'Do not mess this up.'

'The worst she could say is no.'

My heart pounded out of my chest like it never had before. Was I really going to take this chance?

I closed my eyes and took a deep breath as my whole body trembled with butterflies. It was now or never.

As I lowered my gaze to meet hers, her smirk encompassing my vision. I exhaled deeply and said eleven words that would change everything.

'Would you like to go out with me next Saturday night?'

I was petrified, and slightly relieved. That did take some pressure off having spoken the words I had been practicing on the car ride over.

As I looked at her curiously, she played it cool and smiled.

'Oh my god, is this really happening?'

My heart was beating faster than ever before.

'I would love to.'

'Sounds perfect!' I said, not at all losing composure.

Immediately a weight lifted off my shoulders, I felt much more relaxed. My feeling about our connection went from cautiously optimistic to enthralled.

As I had hoped, Aviva agreed to take a chance on me. Soon, it came to be that we would watch Oppenheimer, a three-hour feature. We eventually sat in a Varsity bar in Innaloo, staying sheltered from the cloudy conditions forming outside. We chatted for several hours about our lives and realised we had missed out on so much time together outside of uni. That first date reminds me how powerful genuine conversation can be. It may have been three hours inside that theatre, but it has been many more that I have thought of that night.

Eventually we started dating and have been together nearly three years at the time of writing.

The journey to my current relationship was a rollercoaster of figuring out what I wanted in a partner, as well as learning to be comfortable with who I am. We have grown from close friends to inseparable teammates. Through honest conversations and a willingness to trust each other, we eventually grew our connection to one of strength and unconditional positivity. We have now been together for nearly three years, yet it feels like a lot longer.

There are many reasons why my connection with Aviva makes me happy, the main one being that she provides me with a sense of support whenever I need it. She is never afraid to encourage me and provide me with energy, even if I am not feeling the happiest. That is something you can't put a price on. Her unconditional support and genuine nature give me optimism and hope that I have found the right person for me.

With her, love feels easy. It doesn't make me second guess myself. It is natural and effortless. It feels genuine.

In saying this, no relationship is perfect. We have had many tough conversations about future decisions and values but are always reminded of our shared commitment to each other through the laughter, care and gratitude we continue to practice. My relationship to me feels natural and positive as it makes me calm and steady. That's what matters most, noticing and appreciating those moments.

When in a relationship or searching for that special person, it is very easy to get overwhelmed or feel like you aren't matching society's expectations of romantic excellence. Recently whenever I scroll on Instagram, my algorithm is flooded with pictures of other couples and romantic trends being done for likes and clicks. At times, it honestly feels quite disheartening and overwhelming. By seeing how happy other people are in their relationships, it plants thoughts into my head questioning if I am being the best partner I can possibly be.

Due to the number of romantic comedies that exist, the art of a romantic gesture or grand cliché teaches us that love is an overpowering, all-consuming force. It tells us that love means going above and beyond to be seen. Reality suggests otherwise.

The trends and ideas we see online give us concepts that show what love could look like, but that is one person's experience. In our contemporary landscape, the idea of dating can seem a bit blurrier than once thought. To me, this muddling of dating and romance began with seeing others in happy relationships and wishing the same for myself. Their genuine love and overt display of it made me long for a similar feeling.

I for one felt the need to become performative on social media and cater my profile to a specific niche or interest. The fear of missing out was a large contributor to my general anxiety around relationships and dating. In my experience, I felt a fear of not being in a relationship while others were and this fast-tracked my choice of finding the wrong people until I found the right girl.

Romance and love arrive in the quiet moments, when we learn to fall in love with ourselves first. To properly let our guard down and trust someone else, we must first learn to accept the defining qualities about ourselves. This is a lesson that has taken me many years and many failed attempts to learn, but it is one that has proven to be the most beneficial to me.

Readiness in love is about self-security, not timing or ticking a box. Meaningful love and happiness find you when you stop forcing outcomes. If you become too fixated on the outcome of finding a partner or connecting with someone, this can lead to self-doubt and unhealthy obsession. Love grows in calm, not urgency. This can come through realisations such as becoming more comfortable alone, letting go of chasing validation from others, and love feeling less dramatic and steadier instead. Showing honesty about your flaws, fears and the kind of love you can give doesn't demand perfection. Neither does real love. Real love and connection demands presence. I used to think love was about knowing what to do. Now I realise it's just about showing up.

When it comes to connection, timing matters far more than intensity. You can have a deep connection with someone, but it may not be the right time in your life to engage in it. The challenging experiences of learning about people can allow for the preparation of letting positive love in. When I endured setbacks and rejection from people in my past, I used these as experiences to learn from, understanding what I value in love and connection. These negative experiences informed my journey to becoming fulfilled and truly seen in my own relationship.

For a long time, I saw love as something we chase. It was telegraphed to me that if you didn't find love early, you were somehow behind. But love was never meant to be a race or competition. The older I get, the more I realise that love is less about big moments and more about genuine warmth.

I always thought love was something to figure out.

Now I know it's something I'm still growing into.

CHAPTER TWELVE
LIGHTNING IN A BOTTLE

Do you remember the first time you found something beautiful?

As a child, I always loved the morning drive to school. Not for the scenery or the conversation, but for how those drives would come to shape my future.

On the school commute, our family would typically listen to one of several CD options present in one of my parents' cars. Sometimes it would be something soulful like John Legend or The Jackson 5, other times something more alternative like The Cat Empire or James Blake. It was through these listening parties that my deep love for music would begin to take shape.

Listening to a young Michael Jackson croon over Motown grooves, or hard-hitting synthpop crafted by The Presets often filled me with the joy and happiness that not many other artforms could. Every day, I would always look forward to what sounds would fill my ears each drive to school. It was through these morning drives with Ava and my parents that this connection started to bloom.

To me, music wasn't just something I would hear on the radio and forget about. Every song, every joyful melody spoke to me. Those moments I would listen to pleasant tones through car speakers proved that I was meant to be living in that moment. Each song I heard later became a request, a footnote, a timely reminder of how my greatest love blossomed from tapping my foot in the backseat.

I couldn't quite place my feelings on music as a child.

Was it a deeper passion forming? Was it just something I enjoyed to get through the day? Was it something that simply brought me joy? The validity of my feelings towards music as an artform would later evolve and become more defined over time. What started as innocent moments of curiosity later bloomed into a deeper appreciation of creative artistry.

Each one of us is an artist, whether we would like to admit it or not. Art does not just refer to traditional means of painting, sculpting, or producing. It refers to the process of building and shaping works, ideas and values into tangible real-life missions. We are all artists in how we search for meaning in our lives and in how we set goals. Art may not be exclusively traditional, but it is seen. It is seen in the way we think about what we hold dear, and the way we process emotions or thoughts into a journey.

With every journey, there are hours of work that no one sees. All those nights spent at the computer screen with bleary eyes, all those planning meetings. It all adds up to our goal, our end destination in the problem we are trying to solve. Creativity is not just strictly business though, there is also passion there, enjoyment, a sense of pride and fulfillment in your craft.

Inspiration is not something we can force, it arrives organically. It doesn't wave its hands around and carry bright neon signs, it waits patiently for when the right conditions present themselves. As individuals with unique interests and trajectories, our best ideas often come during moments of intense planning, prep and research.

The main source of creativity in life is being aware. This does not mean just being aware of the things in front of you but being aware in how each decision actively informs your greater plan. For example, if you choose to research for a job in a finance sector, what makes you as a candidate more suited to specific positions than others? What skills or dispositions could you develop to become more accustomed to such a role? The greatest victories and moments of joy come through actively seeking new ways to reach our extraordinary ambitions and unfamiliar opportunities.

Growing up, I often thought everyone's passions came without asking. I figured that one day I would find something I loved almost deservingly. I thought that I would not have to put in any work or research to find something that ignited me and that made me feel energised. It wasn't until the age of eight where I was provided with an opportunity that would change everything.

Whilst attending primary school, I wanted to stand out. I felt as a child that I needed a niche, a way to be different from the rest of the pack. Out of sheer coincidence, my younger sibling Ava was a dancer, quite a talented one. She often danced in competitions as well as private lessons and had proven to be quite the performer.

'Maybe I could try something artistic like Ava too.' I thought.

Knowing of my school's flourishing music and choir program, my parents suggested that I should formally take up an instrument. I was a bit hesitant, as initial piano lessons years prior had not exactly filled me with confidence. But, after a lot of deliberation, I decided to give things a shot.

As I anxiously sat in the front seat of Dad's car reaching the driveway, my anxiety was through the roof. He had heard of a drum school that took students around Perth, helmed by a teacher named Ben. Little did I know it, but Ben would come to be one of my greatest creative influences in life.

After I sheepishly learned about the parts of the drum kit that Saturday morning in his upstairs studio, little murmurings formed in my brain. Maybe, this was the spark I was chasing. Could drumming be that outlet I wanted all along? Initially, I only thought I'd stick with drums for a year and then give it up. Playing an instrument would require too much work and far too much consistency for my eight-year-old brain.

But soon, something changed.

I began to practice playing songs at home to the very same tunes I had first been introduced to on school drives. Drumming didn't feel so chore-like anymore, it became a pleasure. I soon enjoyed practicing songs on the kit and gaining more poise. Hiding behind the drum kit often allowed me to grow confidence in my self-expression, my movement and honestly, my body overall. It felt like I had finally lit a match inside myself to try something new.

My newfound enjoyment of playing the drums led me to performing in recitals held by my drum school, three years going in fact. Thanks to my prior experience in taking drama classes and briefly dabbling in musical theatre, this daunting endeavor proved rewarding.

Soon playing in front of tens led to pretending I was playing in front of millions. I would over the next decade keep honing my craft. My love of drumming also soon changed how I listen to music. I had heard of a streaming service called Spotify from friends and my taste soon sideswiped the usual pop I would hear on the radio. I began digging down rabbit holes of recommendations and letting my tastes form. My growing passion for music later would evolve into attending concerts and a museum-like curation of my digital profile.

That innocent phone call from my parents booking an appointment with Ben was the butterfly effect of all butterfly effects. If that call did not happen, nothing else in this sphere does. That is the biggest thing I have learned from my forays into drumming and music, that the best passions happen by accident. I did not plan on playing an instrument, I planned on finding a spark. The opportunity to play drums fell into my lap, and I decided to try this new opportunity. One by one, those initial lessons turned into practice sessions, recitals and a greater taste for music.

This wider musical identity I formed extended not only from the instrument I played, but also the artists I listened to. My initial playlisting journey began from radio favourites, soundtracks to sporting videogames or songs I would find in YouTube videos by my favourite creators.

I frequently would listen to Australian radio, mainly stations such as Triple J or Mix 94.5, taking mental notes of songs that evoked emotion or groove within me. My yearly experiment of listening to the former's Hottest 100 countdown filled me with names of new artists and tracks to memorise and recite with glee.

In a trip to Europe in 2018, I began to really delve deep into my newfound love for music. When travelling cities such as London, Barcelona, Rome and Athens, I became observant. We would usually visit shopping centres or monuments, often also having hotel television on in the background of our downtime. I decided to keep my ear to the ground and pick up what sounds were popular on the other side of the world. When we strolled the Champs-Elysees, I listened to the brass and jazz playing in eateries and stores. As a result, I made a playlist of the songs and artists that were popular in those foreign cities as a small piece of our trip to take back home.

That Australian summer, I was seeking new songs to practice to on my drumkit. I searched high and low for artists in similar vain to the laid-back, surfy Aussie sound emanating from our local airwaves. I searched through a treasure trove of well-known and lesser seen artists. But one in particular stopped me dead in my tracks.

I clicked play on a song roughly five minutes in length. It was mid-tempo, upbeat and so wonderfully weird. The guitars hummed out melodies like clockwork, and the drums kept a steady groove. The vocals although clearly affected were laidback and reliable. I knew that this was not any other band I had listened to before. It was in this time I would discover a band that would form a large basis of my musical taste and knowledge, The Strokes.

The New York five-piece had me floored in high school. I fell in love with their music and analytically dissected and listened to every song in their catalogue, sometimes multiple times over. It was through discovering their music that I soon began opening my ears to other genres and artists. Frank Ocean, John Mayer, Ball Park Music and Faye Webster are some all-time favourites and acts I owe to my discovery of this band.

In 2020, their album The New Abnormal came out the week I was completing at-home learning due to the COVID pandemic. I awoke at 7am that Friday and listened to the project from start to finish, meticulously taking notes on the things I loved about it the most. From the peppy and upbeat groove on tracks like The Adults Are Talking, to more slower and emotional moments like At The Door, I could tell this album was something I would carry with me as a reminder of the joy music brings. I still have a poster of it hanging on my bedroom wall to this day.

Soon, through my expansive love of music and different genres, I began to entertain the idea of going to concerts. I never used to like loud spaces as a child, often hating loud noises and large crowds. But I could only listen to songs on streaming for so long.

Over the years, I began to take risks as I engaged with my passion outside of my headphones. I soon shared my passion across my state and across continents. Going to concerts with family members and friends became a rite of passage for me. I soon learned of music's unmatched power to bring people together. There is nothing like seeing so many people enjoy the same songs in one place.

I went from playing rhythms from the comfort of my own bedroom to seeing them in live stadiums and auditoriums.

These almost yearly endeavors to see live gigs led me to make passing connection with some of the world's biggest artists. The reason I enjoyed concerts so much wasn't because I knew all the words to songs, but because I knew all the people in that building were enjoying themselves too.

A chance trip to Adelaide, two or three hours from Perth by plane, would lead me to seeing my musical idols in person and up close. Aviva and I had travelled together once before, for a Coldplay gig in Melbourne. It was a joyous experience that reminded me why gigs hold so much power in creating community.

As luck would have it in 2025, The Strokes were set to headline a music festival in Adelaide. Normally, I never would have thought to travel such a way on my own accord. But how could I possibly say no to one of my bucket list experiences?

After months of excitement and hustle as a first-year teacher, I was amped and incredibly excited for our trip. On that October Saturday, the weather had not been particularly kind. I frantically scrolled Instagram and Reddit for updates as Aviva laid out sleeping, blissfully unaware of the stormy conditions outside our hotel window.

'We flew all this way for nothing.' I muttered in an annoyed fashion.

But alas, the storm gave way and we were set to have a fun night. As we trudged through muddy parklands and took our place in the mosh pit, the time could not have moved any slower. After two or so hours of being warmed up by Vance Joy and The War on Drugs, it was go time. The stage techs carefully constructed the band's setup with amps and rows of delicate lighting fixtures. I couldn't believe what I was seeing.

Julian Casablancas and company strolled on stage, bathed in darkness. Tingles of excitement shivered down my entire body. Fifteen-year-old Thomas was running around frantically, twenty-two-year-old me was calm, but conscious of the pandemonium he would soon feel.

From the opening notes of their ninety-minute set, I was transported back to years of memories. I thought of the Year 12 student bursting with excitement when their latest album The New Abnormal blessed my ears for the first time. The times of tapping my feet in the backseat of my parent's cars on school mornings became joyful reminders. I thought back to all those drum lessons and times that music had spoken to me.

I wish I could tell you that I kept my cool and didn't let the moment get to me. It was hard not to feel happy that night. I looked around the open stage and saw people singing lyrics with joy. I saw the band tightly playing with smiles on their faces and knowing they were making thousands of people happy, even if it meant flying many hours across the world to do so.

A rush of adrenaline swept through my body. I had realised that this was a moment in time I was meant to experience. Most importantly of all, I had realised that music was meant to find its way to me. I had chosen the right passion and had been rewarded with unforgettable experiences in turn.

Just like that night, the right passions energise us, they bring a feeling of contentment. I began to grow more comfortable and controlled in my interests is because it felt effortless. I knew that I loved music and that these other arising passions were real because it didn't feel like I had to pretend to like any of it. It felt authentically me. Passion often shows up quietly, when you least expect it.

I did not expect to fall in love with music at a young age, it happened organically. The joy I felt when listening to music came because of everyday experiences and divine convenience. If you truly love something, research it. Make it a part of your routine to dedicate time to your passion. Creativity does not simply come from being stagnant and passive, it comes from wanting to embrace those little moments of change. It comes from accepting that phone call, from writing that to do list. Ambition can only take shape when we give ourselves room to be open minded in exploring new destinations.

Passion we feel in our daily lives comes in the quiet and reflective moments. It shows itself in personal memories and familiar feelings. Music for me has always felt like one of the things that found me before I understood why. Through phases and reflection, it became a constant in my life. Maybe that's all that passion is. It's not screaming at you loudly from across the room. It's not some life-altering sign from the gods suddenly giving you hope. Passion is something that stays with you amongst a world of change.

It can be quite easy to lose sight of the things we enjoy when the outside noise seems too deafening or overbearing.

Harnessing your interests does not always have to be practical, such as going to concerts or making playlists. It can be a mindful exercise just as much. The best way to engage with passion and creativity is to consider just how it will affect and course-chart your daily life.

From feeling invigorated by our deepest passions and interests comes a need to let them be known in the wider world. In today's world, this can often come through social media, recreational groups or even self-led projects or income sources. Celebrating and honing our art lies in accepting its unique nature, to know that the concepts we love too started as accidental moments in time before they became something greater.

Next time you find yourself in a moment that you feel may be monumental, stop yourself. Mentally note take how you feel in that moment, take note of what is going on around you. Consider exactly what about this moment in time makes it so impactful to your story. Is it the people around you? The space you are in? The mode of work you are consuming?

Let it sit and fester before you turn that spark into something greater. Channel your freedom to create new ideas in those quiet moments. You never know where those unseen hours and small realisations will lead you.

Capture those small moments like lightning in a bottle.

CHAPTER THIRTEEN
A LITTLE BIRDIE TOLD ME

I sat in the library, staring around at the dimly lit rows of books and passersby.

The words just wouldn't come out.

The blueprint was there, my notes dictating the structure for each chapter and the direction I wanted this story to go. But, I couldn't articulate those thoughts to paper. Writing a book was supposed to be a lifelong dream come true, instead it felt more like an exercise in self-doubt and questioning every little decision.

My chest tightened. My palms shook. And then, it spoke. 'Why would anyone read your book?'

'No one is going to take you seriously.'

'Stop trying to sound deep.'

For a library nestled in the heart of one of Perth's most populous residential areas, the silence in the room was almost taunting me. That voice spoke louder than I thought possible.

Those words uttered did not come from a nearby onlooker, but from my own head. As the hours ticked by on that February afternoon, my mind began to tire. I had been sitting at this booth since 11am, telling myself I couldn't leave until I drafted yet another chapter. The ticking wasn't from a clock, but inside my mind. The beat of the music in my headphones pulsed even louder, the vocals turning into warbled non-descript noise. I had to stay true to my deadlines, but I couldn't rush my vision.

I walked around the library upon entering that morning, taking careful time to scan the aisles while the staff greeted me with a friendly and curious smile. As I scanned the rows of books my mind began to talk yet again.

'You'll never make something that good.'

'Your book will never be read at a library like this.'

'Why are you wasting your time on this project?'

As I sat in that cozy library booth, I began to consider whether I was doing right by myself in writing a book. I began to question whether people would gravitate or learn anything from my story. In my mind, I was just another naive storyteller hoping to reach an audience. Slowly I looked at the time on my screen. Minutes flew by.

12:30pm.

1:24pm.

2:00pm.

2:45pm.

3:00pm.

Hours had passed, music still played in my ears. Not one word had appeared on my page. I lowered my head, almost in embarrassment at the time I had spent procrastination rather than working on my masterpiece. My inner voice had been chattering for hours, and I just let it keep talking down to me.

I hastily shut my laptop and packed my bag, streaming out of the library at a speed akin to an Olympic power walker. I have never driven home with such a hurry.

On the drive home, my thoughts spiraled. My inner critic questioned whether I was ready to write a book, if a twenty-something year old had wisdom the best authors could conjure up in their sleep. I became fixated on knowing why my inner critic was so powerful, and why it manifested itself in the quietest of arenas.

The library became my second home when writing this book, I often went there for a change of environment and a chance to write in a different environment. It was always so nice to be surrounded by a calming, soothing room where people came to read and take time to research or explore new things about our world.

Only I couldn't remain calm. I couldn't switch off.

The voice never ceased, even when every other part of me did.

As I lay awake that night, I tossed and turned as I was trapped by my bedsheets, nowhere to go in trying to escape these thoughts. I had to let them sit. As I stared up at the ceiling, I began to wonder if maybe my head was right.

'What if no one cared what I have to say?'

'What if the book I wrote didn't reach people?'

'What if people thought I was trying to be someone I wasn't?'

I finally shut my eyes around midnight, the hum of passing cars outside not nearly being as provoking as the constant babbling coming from inside me.

The next morning when I sat down to write again, the critic kept up its direct and no-nonsense tone.

'These chapter ideas are too vague, where's the substance?'

'Who wants to hear yet ANOTHER lecture about anxiety?'

This voice was not seen, rather heard. It lied in the shadows and presented itself when the opportunity arose. It feasted on causing pressure to those it inhabits.

This voice does not sound like anyone I know, yet it always finds exactly the right cutting words. It is a judge ruling us as being down and out before we even try. I like to think the inner critic is a commentator watching a sporting event, picking apart and narrating on each misstep we make. Our inner critic is informed by negative biases we hold about ourselves as well as past difficult experiences. What we think comes from what we live through.

My inner voice wanted me to achieve the best grades, see myself as untouchable and only make good decisions. It quite often lamented my actions or experiences when things didn't go well. This voice talked in extreme examples to convince me I wasn't quite where I ought to be.

For days and weeks even, I would stare at my screen for hours.

I would procrastinate. I would ruminate.

Not a single word would be written.

I would shut my laptop and miss out on yet another opportunity to create.

My inner critic has never failed to keep me on my toes. Sometimes for better, sometimes for the worst. Some days my inner critic would stop me from doing the things I set out to. If I wanted to go to the gym, it would tell me I was too tired. If I wanted to study or search for work, it would tell me it wasn't worth it.

At some of the most important times in my life, the inner critic has shown up to give me a daunting reality check of my inner feelings.

When I received my ATAR Results in 2020 after graduating Year 12, I was anything but relieved. I was on holiday in Mandurah, anxiously awaiting to see whether the hours of final study in Year 12 had paid off.

I dried myself off after taking in some sunshine at a local beach. I wrapped myself in a beach towel and waddled into the bedroom I was occupying. I hastily searched for my login to access my results.

My entire body shivered. This was a moment over a decade in the making.

I couldn't bear the suspense.

I finally had access to the results, this was the moment of truth. I closed my eyes, exhaled, and pressed the login button to the student portal.

I opened my eyes, looked down, and sat still.

Not a single breath.

Nothing said out loud.

Only silence. Only panic.

This was not the ending I had anticipated.

I was shellshocked.

My entire body quivered in fear. The gigantic boldened number loomed on my screen as a stark reminder of how far I had fallen short of my expectations.

'That is a terrible ATAR.'

'This is all you could manage?'

'What was even the point of studying for exams if you bombed out like this?'

I hung my head in shame and stayed locked in my room for the remainder of the evening, only making a brief appearance to scoff down some fish and chips as a means of eating away my sorrows.

Tears began to stream down my face ever so quickly as I threw my phone across the room. In my schooling, I craved validation and wanted to be the absolute best at everything I encountered. Perfection was the answer and there was no substitute. By the fear of failure I instilled in myself, I was embarrassed to admit when I would slip up or make a mistake. Receiving a sub-par ATAR was to me the ultimate embarrassment.

The fear of not being good enough, was a common school of thought. My inner critic tended to expose itself more during the most negative experiences. The times I failed were not moments, but precedents. Just because I didn't pass that test or because I bombed in that job interview, my mind convinced me the same would likely to occur each time.

My inner critic was talking so loudly because it was attempting to defend me from feeling regret or shame. It thought that because I had faced negativity in the past, those same or similar experiences should be shunned in favour of safe or comfortable ones.

At family events my inner critic became louder and louder as the years passed. Every morning would turn into a smattering of changing outfits, staring at myself in the mirror, and mentally preparing conversation starters with people I had known since I came into this world. I always loved catching up with family for birthdays, holidays, or even just casual gatherings. But due to my own internal expectations, they became much more weighted than they appeared.

When I would talk to cousins, aunties or uncles, I would attempt to respond to questions with a sincere sense of humour, often trying to distract from the fact I didn't feel I had anything going on worth talking about. As I would eat homemade food and look around at a sea of communally happy faces, one thought began to repeat.

Every. Single. Event.

'I don't match up to everyone else.'

All I knew was that these thoughts made it harder for me to feel comfortable around people who knew me better than most. I had no ill will towards anyone but myself. My mind, these intrusive, exaggerated distortions about myself, were bringing me down, and stripping away the confidence I had been building in myself through diligent practice.

The very same thoughts at family events incessantly repeated themselves as I scanned the library each afternoon I visited. They no longer appeared in isolation, but on a consistent basis to remind me that I couldn't ignore them any longer.

I never quite understood my inner critic's intentions until I began to embrace mindfulness and write down my thoughts. I would write down every single thought I would have about myself. One by one I would evaluate each one and its relevance. It was through this practice that I stumbled across a frank revelation. My inner critic thinks it was protecting me. Protecting me from failure, from making a fool of myself, from feeling heartbreak.

As I reflect on my experience drafting this book, a thought comes to mind.

The reason I had those thoughts was not because I truly believed them, but because I was finding excuses not to continue. I let my tiredness, my fatigue take over. I knew in the back of my mind that I truly wanted to complete this project, and I started it for a reason. However, my mind was finding any reason possible to make me second guess my creativity.

Why?

It demanded perfection.

My inner critic spoke so loudly because it knew that I was capable of making something genuinely interesting, and that I couldn't let myself down. I had to convince my brain to push through the noise and keep my view squarely on what was necessary.

Although I persevered and eventually completed the story you are now reading, it did not come without setbacks. My inner voice conjured up visions of glory and excellence, while creating a brutal comedown of regret when those unreal expectations are not achieved. The inner critic inside me didn't want me to fail, but instead to work hard in achieving my goals.

Even in this very moment as I continue to write this book, I am still plagued with thoughts and hinderances questioning if each page is strong enough.

My mind won't dare settle for anything less than what I truly want.

It must be stressed that our inner critic is not something that will be eradicated. Self-doubt will of course always be present, it is inevitable. The key to quietening your inner critic is through training it. You don't destroy it outright, you help build it from a different lens.

Think back to all the times you received negative feedback. Maybe that interview didn't go how you hoped, maybe your monthly performance review at your sales job wasn't the most positive.

The best way to train your inner critic is to look at things from a constructive lens. When your inner voice tries to bring you down, recognise the thought. Let it sit. Then, question it. Is this thought true, what evidence is there? Then, replace the voice. Instead of saying 'I can't do this, it's too hard.' Try saying, 'I can't do this yet, but I am learning and there is always room to try again.'

By training the inner critic, you are actively trying to fight the negative thoughts in your brain. This practice of questioning, reflecting and reconstructing can take some time, but it is necessary in being able to shut out those negative beliefs and chase the outcomes you truly want.

My inner critic isn't an almighty overlord. It is a voice that thinks it knows. It encouraged me to analyse my thoughts and encounter them face to face. My inner voice allowed me to actively challenge and consider the ways I spoke to myself. The critic broadcasted the areas in which I hated myself, where I was trying to fit into places it didn't deem I fit into. As hurtful as those internal monologues were, the frequency at which they spoke diminished through time.

That voice still chirps. It still claims I am not good enough. The change now is that I choose to confront it. I simply stop. I reflect. I question.

The voice still talks.

I just don't hand it the mic anymore.

CHAPTER FOURTEEN
THINGS I NEVER FINISHED

I have started a lot of things in my life. Podcasts. Websites. Plans that looked good on paper but went nowhere once novelty wore off.

At the start of 2025, I sought to give myself a clear direction for the next few years. My cycle of starting things but never truly finishing them led to the creation of a four-year plan. I wanted to truly take charge of my life rather than letting it pass me by.

I wrote on a piece of paper some aspirations I had, my own bucket list if you will. Then, I worked backwards. For example, with my goal of teaching in the UK. That was the finished article, that was the destination.

In the interim my goals are applying for positions at Perth schools, building a reputation, making a steady income and stable home life. Then, when the other cogs are in order, the time may come to approach a recruiter who specialises in such travel plans, or research specific schools I would want to work at in England.

Success used to mean stellar grades and unabashed confidence in myself. Now, it means giving my best in all pursuits and staying true to myself no matter what.

As a teenager specifically, I struggled strongly with ego and belief in myself. When I would achieve something positive, such as getting a good grade in a test or assignment, I would often see myself as superior to others and think of myself as being smarter. I let success get to my head, I let it change the way I saw other people in my life. I was channeling creativity and chasing my goals in a selfish and egotistical way. I was trying to step on the necks of others to reach my ambitions rather than approaching things with a more wholesome attitude.

Through intense honest conversations and journalling sessions, I soon realised around the start of university that I needed to change my ways. I could no longer survive by trying to beat all comers to reach the top. I had to learn to be more of a libertarian and to acknowledge and support others. I was caught in two minds of questioning if I should serve myself or help others conquer their own journeys. Eventually, I came to a healthy compromise. I could still chase my ambitions and want success for myself while still supporting those who loved me.

Inspiration can strike you in any place. The inspiration for this book struck me on a European holiday several years ago. Being creative is not exclusively for the six figure influencers or the Wall Street entrepreneurs. It is for us all.

Some of my areas of enthusiasm include music history, football tactics and art. Your niche can be something very specific and personal to you.

I consistently research and scour the internet for musicians' creative advice on how they make a song, or the aesthetic of an album. Everything takes time and process. Through trial and error, I have started and retracted many projects to chase my personal mission of making the world a better place.

Often my project ideas would take place in the form of media, including a YouTube channel and several podcasts. I did not receive intrinsic benefit, but felt these projects were necessary to feel a part of wider cultural discussion on things I was passionate about.

When I graduated high school, I started my own mental health project. I had a full website, a formally produced podcast with meaning, and a goal of providing access to mental health services across Australia. On the surface, this project had all the makings to be a success. A month after I launched it, I sat on my hands and became complacent. I had revealed the project, the website, the podcast. But it was just a name, a brand, an excuse to get my name out.

These ideas were ambitions sure, but they became self-serving and were not given the proper time and dedication to grow.

It wasn't until sitting through days of boredom and low-energy that I had enough. I couldn't let days pass me by and keep torching myself by refusing to act on my ideas. I had to create a sustainable future of myself, and as such, began to roadmap the next few years of my life.

This desire to act fast very nearly caused a dramatic change of course in my life.

At the end of 2025, I almost moved to the UK for a year in pursuit of teaching. I was caught in a spot of limbo with my future in Perth deeply uncertain. I knew that I had to find another option and fast. I was in back-and-forth communication with a recruiter to make this move possible. I had my heart set on beginning my new life in London. For weeks, I went every which way in my mind determining whether I was completely ready for such a major life transition. The reality was that I still lived at home and did not have as much independence as such a lifestyle change would need.

Thanks to my prior experience travelling to Europe with family, I seriously entertained this possibility. I wanted to walk the streets of Kensington, to watch football at Wembley, to ride the London Eye. It would mean the world to me to return to a place that had given me so many memories as a teenager.

I kept the idea a secret from everyone but a few close family members and Aviva. I wanted this moment to feel monumental for not only myself, but others too. I wanted this move to feel like I was finally breaking out on my own. This was my great chance.

After initial uncertainty, I went full speed ahead researching rental prices in London, specific areas I would live in, flight costs, and many other factors. I had travelled to London multiple times as a teenager and had fallen in love with the city. As an avid enjoyer of English culture, it seemed like a natural fit for me.

Weeks went by, I was caught in two minds at work. On one hand I was focused on my immediate job teaching Year 3 in Perth, a job which I for the most part enjoyed. The other side of the coin was that my dream move abroad was still firmly on my mind.

I had to make this happen.

Late October came and it was nearing decision time, if I wanted to move to the UK, a January 2026 move was my best shot to fall in line with their second semester. But for some reason, there was something holding me back from making such a huge decision.

Fear. Fear of the unknown.

I was planning to pretty much uproot my whole life and put myself in a completely foreign country, with differing culture and new ways of living. I didn't consider just how much adjustment and growth would need to be made. I had thought of the excitement of starting something new, of taking steps away from my comfortable life in Perth. I had only looked at the bright spots, not the full picture.

So, I came to a compromise.

I sat in my room after days of consulting my parents about my decision. I had to be realistic and think about what would suit me best. I had family, friends and goals at home, I couldn't just drop them all in a flash. I would never forgive myself for making such a drastic change with such little notice.

I had to wait until the time was right.

The dream had to be put on hold, at least for now.

Travelling is still a goal of mine, and a hobby I particularly enjoy. Not just to Europe, but all across Australia too. This avenue of travel was just not quite right for me yet.

It hurt to realise that my dream would have to be postponed, but it made me feel happy in knowing I could prepare myself for it in the meantime. I could do plenty of research about costs, areas to live and quality of life. I also could spend more time with the people I have in Perth and make even more memories.

The idea was created.

The hope was there.

The timing just wasn't right.

As much as it stung, it was something I had to deal with. Even though I couldn't immediately chase my dream of living in England, I could still chase other goals and make meaningful change in many other ways. There was still unfinished business I needed to attend to, finding my creative lane.

If you aren't quite sure just what the area is that gives you that spark, self-audit yourself. Write down a list of skills, passions and lived experiences that really resonate with you. These are the areas you will find strike a chord with you as being authentically and uniquely you. Identify what you genuinely love, even what you are good at.

Make yourself uncomfortable.

Brainstorming new ideas and creative interests comes from

trial and error. It wasn't until I first learned to play the drums and took a risk by learning a new instrument that I let music consume a large part of my life. Music became a core passion of mine through making myself uncomfortable in undergoing new experiences.

Currently sitting in front of me at my desk is my daily routine. This routine helps me achieve some key goals, these being to exercise more, to become more social in my life, and to actively seek out work to earn an income. My daily routine helps keep myself in check by actively working towards each of these goals in a low-key and deliberate manner.

It took years of internal overthinking to nail down a solid routine to keep me productive.

My dilemma was never coming up with better ideas. It was if I was man enough to finally follow through.

CHAPTER FIFTEEN
SAVOURING THE MOMENT

You don't know what you've got until it's gone.

2025 was a year of transition for me. In the span of weeks, I graduated university, began a new career path, and moved house for the very first time. It was the latter of these three that was the most difficult life change.

From 2003 until 2025, we had lived in a house in Dianella. Salamander Street was a busy, quaint street with friendly neighbours and a real warm feeling. Number 13 was not just a home to me, but a place where I first started to find myself.

The memories I had built in that house were countless. From the playdates with friends where we'd splash around in the pool, or Christmases and gatherings spent with loved ones. It is easy to see why it came as such a shock to me when Mum announced in December of 2024 that we would be moving to another house in the suburb.

Our house had its problems, every home does. But this was the place where I lived out my childhood. I wasn't ready to give it up and let some other hands touch a lifetime of memories.

On a near daily basis, I argued with my Mum and Ava, contesting their excitement to change locations.

'Why do we have to move? This house is perfect!'

'It's unfair that we have to suddenly pack our things.'

My initial reaction to this sudden announcement was anger and pure irritation. I would do everything I can to fight back and somehow change Mum's mind of moving house.

Daily conversations turned to tears and shouting matches. I shouted and threw my weight around if we could stay in our home that had meant too much to me.

The days kept ticking by as my resistance never wavered. I wrote down a laundry list of reasons as to why we should stay and stared at it for hours.

As a boy, I often dismissed my life circumstances. I thought attending private school and living in a nice house surrounded by family that cared about me was normal.

Becoming grounded was something I had struggled with quietly as I grew older and graduated high school. Due to my place of privilege and having a relatively easy upbringing, I often negated the fact that others I knew might not have things as comfortable, and that their version of comfortable could look drastically different.

When Mum told us we would be moving house in two months, my ego would not let me come to terms with such a decision. I kicked up an almighty fuss and protested that my home and its memories were being suddenly taken away without a second thought.

Moving after two decades in one home was always going to have its challenges. I wasn't ready to let go of my bedroom, the times of running around the backyard, the many acrobatic jumps into our pool, causing water to splatter all over our fence and cars.

But there was no Hail Mary pass that I could throw to make this decision reverse, it was set in stone.

I would have to say goodbye to my first home.

This decision did not sit right with me for weeks.

I couldn't take my mind off the sudden change and how I felt my perspective wasn't being considered.

At that point in my life, I had just completed my university degree and actively searching for my first teaching job. It felt like I was already facing a mountain of change in my professional life, I didn't know how much more change I could really handle.

Mum noticed I was feeling quite worked up and spoke to me one night about the change.

'Tom, I know you are going through a lot right now. You are dealing with change of your own.'

'I know that it is hard to say goodbye to this house, but it has problems, we can't afford to keep pumping money into it.'

'I'm not asking you to be okay with it, but could you please just work with me to ensure we can make the move light on everyone?'

I nodded but didn't fully agree.

Even if I wasn't genuinely excited about moving, I still needed to be grateful and keep myself in check. This new house wasn't just moving from place to place, it symbolised a new era for me, a chance to make my mark in a new area of my life. I was due to walk across the graduation stage a few days before moving house, slowly dipping my toes in the water of adulthood.

With change came putting the wheels in motion. I began to pack up my bedroom and all my belongings at home. As I piled things into cardboard boxes, I came to an important realisation. This wasn't goodbye, this was just a chance to take my life to new places.

I packed old books and magazines in, reminding me of those moments as a child I would read up on the latest football scores and transfers.

I packed away old toys, a remnant of my childhood when I learned how to express myself through play.

I packed away my clothes, each article representing a day where I wore personalities, not outfits.

One January morning, I made the ever so tough five-minute commute from our old place to our new place. Immediately, I began to pick holes in our future home. It was on the corner of the street, it was a smaller block, the prospect of an empty bedroom needing to be filled created dread in my mind.

I stepped through the doorway of our new place for the first time, greeted by an excitable real estate agent. As lovely as he was, I was seething that this change was truly happening.

Stepping through that doorway was the reality.

Stepping into a new chapter was confronting.

As I scanned the house, I began to take note of every little thing that was different to our old place. I commented on the space of the bedrooms, the fact one of us would be sleeping in a room right next to the front door.

My inner critic would not stop finding ways to nit-pick and examine every square inch of our soon to be home.

As unhealthy as this thinking was, it painted a clear picture.

I needed to get out of my head.

Soon, weeks passed and I slowly worked myself into accepting the move. I began to research our new place online, looking at images of each room and thinking about how they might be used. When discussing the new place with my cousins,

I began to fake my optimism and speak with excitement, almost tricking myself into feeling positively about the change.

As moving day approached my stepdad Theo and I had spent the previous days hauling boxes between places in his work van. It was through these journeys from house to house that I came to realise the excitement of this opportunity. This was a chance to start fresh and make something new of my life.

I was in a period of great stress at the time, so naturally I chose to focus on the negatives. I should have been focusing on the positives, the fact we get to move to a new, clean, spacious home. Yes, there were many memories made at Number 13, but there would be just as many made at our new place. That is an exciting change.

We eventually moved into our new place, still in Dianella. In spending more time at the new house as weeks went by, I soon became used to my surroundings and came to realise I was worrying over nothing all along. My new home was a place where I could learn to be myself and build from the ground up.

It was time to make a change.

For good.

Being thankful is a vital part of growth. Thankfulness allows us to better reflect on the things we are afforded and be grateful for the ways in which we can support those around us. By being stripped of the luxuries we desire, we appreciate the ordinary things we have always around us. Gratitude doesn't show up in the loud moments when things are chaotic, it shows itself in the quiet, calm occasions when rest and reflection is needed. Learning to be thankful means embracing our circumstances and showing up when we would rather stay complacent.

In the end, nothing about the new house changed.

Just the way I was looking at it.

I thought I was losing something.

I wasn't.

I was just being asked to let go of one version of my life, so I could embrace the next with open arms.

What I learned is that it wasn't my home I was holding onto, but the boy who lived inside.

LETTING THE LIGHT IN

I once had a best friend.
He was warm, excitable and always ready to make you feel like the most important person in the world.
This friend didn't have two legs, instead four.
We would spend moments in our backyard throwing and chasing a tennis ball.
I would ride his back like a horse around our garden, I would swim with him on warm summer days.
He would accompany me on walks around the park and trips to the shops.
There was something simple about it.
He didn't need much to be happy, just time and presence.
We lost him many years ago.
The other week I found him again.
In old photo albums.
The same trademark smile and innocent eyes.
The same feeling I had as a boy, chasing his tail in circles.
For a moment nothing changed.
The backyard was still there.
The rusty shed.
The afternoons that felt like they would never end.
He did not live a long life.
But the time we shared stayed with me.
I see him now in small moments.
In quiet ones.
In the kind of joy you don't have to chase.
No one could replace him.
No one will.
He wasn't just a friend.
He was Harry.

CHAPTER SIXTEEN
TO BE CONTINUED

I didn't think I would ever write a book.

Yet here it is.

I was told I would have very little chance of even being here from the jump. But through hope and immense support, I lived to tell the tale.

When I look back on my life so far, I look back with great fondness. I know not everything went to plan, but I am okay with that. The obstacles, the anxieties, the roadblocks were put in my path to shape the man I am becoming.

I thought only people with great success stories could share the tale of their ascent to greatness. I never knew each one of us possess the same greatness many of our idols do.

Writing this book has forced me to look at myself in ways I never did before. It compelled me to examine the happy moments that brought me joy, the days that I found tough but soldiered on anyways.

It tested me in ways I didn't expect. Days of doubt, frustration and hesitation shadowed my work. Yet revisiting the most difficult days brought clarity. Every misstep and every disappointment was a lesson. Every small joy brought me back to who I am. I was encouraged to examine my entire life so far and capture my perfect story.

This story was not destined to be perfect in its events or outcomes, but perfect in its honesty. My story is honest in the fact that it is unfinished. It contains moments where I was close to giving up on my dreams, to settling for less than I first chased.

I am human because I embrace awkwardness.

I am human because I strive to be better.

In writing this book, I sought to explain my past in the most authentic way possible. I went back to photo albums, had conversations with close family members about specific memories, and carried a wealth of experiences I could weave into the fabric of these pages.

I also went back to places that bought me joy, where those formative memories were made. These journeys were emotional, yet stark reminders of how far I have come.

I recently went back to Light Street Reserve, the same park that I had strolled through as a happy child many years ago. Light Street wasn't just a park to me, it was a place to be with my thoughts and embrace nature's beauty.

Not too long ago, I often came here to shoot hoops. To play cricket in the nets. To talk and chat with friends and family.

I would come here when I felt happy to get some sunlight.

I would come here when frustrated to seek clarity.

But that day, it felt different. It felt exciting.

As I visited my sanctuary, the streets were quiet, but the internal excitement was deafening.

Whilst an assortment of songs tickled my eardrums, I noticed my surroundings.

I could see leaves trembling in the breeze, the sunlight dashing across the many hectares of grass, a new breed of locals playing in the wilderness I had seen years before.

Cars zoomed by on the busy streets as I nodded at strangers passing by with a wry smile. I beamed with joy like I felt when I was smaller, knowing that a place I hadn't visited in some time still meant so much to me.

To many, it was just a block of land filled with trees, bush and footpaths. To me, it was a place I could go and journey through my thoughts.

It was a place I could go to make everything feel okay when it felt like it would never be.

That day, I felt like a little kid again running through the wide footy oval. The wave of happiness I felt in my body was unlike anything else I could describe.

Just like that, Light Street felt like home again.

In reflecting, I never quite knew which version of me was writing the story.

I never knew who Thomas Robertson really was.

Finishing this book doesn't feel like an ending, a conclusion to a story. It feels like standing still for the first time in a while.

I don't have things figured out.

I didn't think my story was remarkable.

However, I have learned over the past twenty-three years that what makes a story remarkable isn't plot twists or character shifts, it's creating a story that is genuine.

I didn't hesitate because I doubted what I had to say.

I hesitated because I didn't think I was ready to say it.

Still at age 23, I don't have my life together.

Honestly, nor do I want to.

I keep getting back up and trying again.

The old me would shy away, find excuses not to create something that can challenge or shape people.

The real me would stand up, look my doubt dead in the eyes and carry on smiling.

I'm not afraid anymore, it's taken years of practice to realise maybe I never was.

Twenty-three years - not a messy painting, but a journey of ups, downs, countless lessons. I close my eyes, comforted that I am still learning what my best looks like. My story - this story - is just taking shape.

My journey is nowhere near over.

The rest, I still have to conquer.

WHAT I KNOW NOW

Here are some lessons that I have learned along twenty-three years of growing, reflecting and changing.

1. At times, everything felt like it was going wrong. Most of it had to happen.
2. I kept comparing my path to everyone else's. It's in the doubt, reflection and questioning where I learned the most.
3. Losing people doesn't mean you failed. It means you are growing in different directions.
4. I spent too long trying to fix a body that was never broken.
5. The things I cared about didn't come when I forced them. They showed up when I stopped trying so hard.
6. Knowing what you want from someone matters. Knowing what you want from yourself matters more.
7. I hate how much I overthink. It usually means I care more than I admit.
8. My inner voice used to feel like a judge. Now it feels like something I can challenge.
9. Saying thank you isn't just polite. It's a reminder not to take things for granted.
10. I didn't realise how much my family shaped me until I began to step away from it.

11. Every time I compared my life, it felt smaller. It never actually was.

12. No one was coming to figure it out for me. I had to start.

ACKNOWLEDGEMENTS

Writing this book has been a journey like no other. I couldn't have done it alone.

To my immediate family, Mum, Dad, Ava, Tom and my grandparents. Thank you for embracing all sides of me: silly, happy, frustrated. It is your consistent love that has truly kept me going in chasing my dreams. Thank you for the lessons and continued encouragement. Your support and willingness to lend an ear means more than I can properly say. I am incredibly grateful for the family I was born into.

To my wider family and relatives – thank you for always showing up – for listening when I needed to share my crazy thoughts. Catching up and simply spending time together has created some of my happiest memories. Those moments shaped this book more than I probably realise. The family I have been fortunate enough to have constantly reminds me that connection is one of the most important things we have.

To Aviva – thank you for consistently being my energy on the days I have none. Your warmth, compassion and generosity bring me more happiness than I thought possible. I love you for all that you have given me - and all that you will.

To my high school brothers – the boys I shared six years of my life with. It's hard to explain how much of an impact our community has had on me. Being a man for others taught me about compassion and service without ego. Thank you to the boys who believed in me on days I didn't believe in myself. Thank you for the laughs, the encouragement, and the banter.

To my teachers –- thank you for encouraging me to follow in your passion for inspiring others. It is because of you that I am stepping into the job I was born to do, teaching. I hope to set the same example you set for the shy kid hoping to find himself.

Lastly, to you, the reader. Thank you for taking a chance on my story just as I took a chance in writing it. May it inspire you to meet yourself honestly and shine your light.

Maybe we'll meet again soon.

For more details about this book, visit:

www.thomasrobertson.com.au